BEYOND
THE
FENCE

BEYOND
THE
FENCE:
Converging Memoirs

AMANDA EPPLEY &
JOHN HOURIHAN

BEYOND THE FENCE: CONVERGING MEMOIRS

iUniverse books may be ordered through booksellers or by contacting:

iUniverse
1663 Liberty Drive
Bloomington, IN 47403
www.iuniverse.com
1-800-Authors (1-800-288-4677)

ISBN: 978-1-4917-8285-9 (sc)
ISBN: 978-1-4917-8286-6 (e)

Library of Congress Control Number: 2015918567

Print information available on the last page.

iUniverse rev. date: 11/13/2015

TABLE OF CONTENTS

PREFACE

How do you explain the filth of war to your adult children?

How do you explain the fire of your 21st century social causes to your 20th century parents?

So many of the soldiers of Vietnam came home to people who didn't want to understand what had happened in southeast Asia even at the time, so forty-five years later how do you explain why you still stand up and fight only when it is needed? In 2015 how do you explain to your elders why you feel it is more important to go into the inner cities to teach, carrying a $45,000 a year degree from the number one college in the country, than to nestle into the comfort and safety of the suburbs?

There is a reason we generations don't understand each other. We seldom communicate, and when we do we hardly listen. I found out during the first years of my retirement that, first you let them know who you were and who you are. Then you listen to what their wars were like. Sometime during that time I found a way.

This joint memoir of two people, one a 69 year old decorated Vietnam vet, one a thirty-something pacifist, Teach for America inner-city teacher and champion of equal rights for all, shows how two very different people can find out how much they have in common and how each can ultimately understand the viewpoint of the other. It is how we learn from history and keep it from repeating itself. It is how we find the American Dream.

To that end we wrote "Beyond the Fence."

INTRODUCTION

This is the story of two lives, beginning thirty years apart, unfolding in dual narrative vignettes in chronological juxtaposition, creating a clear mosaic of how a family can achieve the American Dream the way it was always intended, the way it is still possible.

He spent three tours in Vietnam, and he refused to carry a weapon.

"I'm not coward, Sarge. Ask around. I'm not asking to go home. I'll stay here and do my job. I'll die for my country. I just won't kill for it anymore."

She taught in Oakland, and as a New England small-town white girl she connected with her inner-city students of color over the needless death of one of their own.

"My first year teaching, which culminated at the funeral, shattered my comfort zone, ... I had finally found what my travels, my moves, my different professions and degrees had failed to produce. My students offered me a window to a world beyond my own, pulled back the thick drapes, and explained it to me. I will be forever grateful for their patience and their respect."

He was born into the poorest family in town.

She was born into middle-class America.

He moved at age ten to south Phoenix, where he survived knife fights, picking cotton and being the white kid in a Mexican barrio.

She grew up in suburbia with an in-ground pool and a golden retriever, and with parents marking time to their inevitable divorce.

He received a blank diploma from high school.

She was a valedictorian from the same school.

He joined the Army and went to Southeast Asia to pay for a state college education.

She studied at elite institutions and travelled the country with a Frisbee.

He raised a son and a daughter.

She is raising two sons.

Part One

CHILDHOOD

Chapter 1
BEYOND THE FENCE

(John, 3 years old)

1949: Britain recognizes the independence of the Republic of Ireland; the state of Vietnam is formed; the first practical rectangular TV tube is announced; the first 45 rpm records are sold.

In the late 1940s, the cedar-shingled, four-room hovel a quarter-mile off the road into the woods on the North Purchase with the broken furnace and the irritable plumbing system, in the then small factory town of Milford, Massachusetts, had been a step up. It had been a major ascension from my vision of the city streets of Worcester from the second-story tenement window above the railroad tracks when I was three years old, but I still screamed like the devil when we moved there.

Worcester had my comfortable sunny spot and my railroad tracks. As far as I was concerned it was hard to move up from that.

Out the gray back door, down the rickety, outside, paint-peeling wooden stairs, at the end of the grass, dirt and colored-glass pieces in our backyard, in the heart of the low-end center of the city, where the rail cars click-clacked slowly past the brickyard, the plumbing supply store, the Irish bars, the Greek market, and our yard, there was a fence. But it was a fence that couldn't stop school children headed across the tracks to St. Peter's school, never mind a three year old Irish urchin who had passed the terrible twos with flying colors and spent late mornings crawling backwards down the hill, under the fence, toward the tracks of what was probably the Grafton-Upton railroad, eager to see the "wide wide world."

I liked the wind in my face, from the train as it flew by only feet away.

I scurried toward the tracks. I knew how far away to sit. It was where the pale yellow scrub grass, that reached to the top of my head as I crawled, met the gravel. I would sit just a few body lengths off the edge of the big dark brown creosote covered wooden ties, play with the gravel, and wait for the train.

I liked the wind. It excited me.

One of the last things I remember about the city, before we moved to the woods, was spending the mornings in the room that had no furniture, in a sunny spot on the hardwood floor, in my soft and warm diaper with a Zwieback biscuit until the sun moved enough so that the spot crawled up the wallpaper. Having had enough comfort, I would go out to feel the wind.

The engineer stopped the train one morning, actually hissed the great coal-black locomotive to a stop just before he got to me, climbed out of the engine cabin, and swung down onto the gravel with a crunch.

"You live up there in that house?" he asked, nodding toward my house.

I don't remember answering him. In my family, even at three, we knew we didn't hang out third-story windows, play with sticks, put things in the wall plugs or talk to strangers, and we especially didn't tell them where we lived.

I followed him up to the house and listened while he shouted at my mother. I knew that was probably not a good idea, for him. He had the intestinal fortitude to shout right in the face of Sweet Genevieve, who listened intently, then laughed softly, a lock of her soft brunette hair falling over her sad brown eyes.

"He likes the wind," she answered. Then she must have mentioned something about what her husband Scrapper Jack would do to him if she told, and he left as fast as he had arrived. Climbed back into his train, let out a hiss of relief, and left.

"Don't go down there anymore," she said to me as she picked me up and swung me from her left hand to her right, a practiced move she had perfected with my four older sisters and would use later with both my younger brothers.

I rested my head on her shoulder. "God knows there are better ways to feel the wind."

When we moved to Milford on my fourth birthday, I was bribed out of my hysteria with a red-cased record player and a 33 rpm of "**The Old Chisholm Trail.**" Woody Guthrie being my old man's favorite.

And therefore mine.

Chapter 2
WHERE'S THE GARAGE?

(Mandy, 3 years old)

1979: The Iran Hostage Crisis begins; Soviet troops invade Afghanistan, prompting the U.S. boycott of the following summer's Olympics; "Video Killed the Radio Star" is released.

It was 1979 when we moved to a three bedroom split-level home on Marked Tree Road in the upscale town of Holliston, Massachusetts, a far cry from the confining walls of the tiny home in Uxbridge we had put forever behind us.

It was one month before I turned three, and I thought we had moved to the jungle as I fought my way through the outstretched arms of grasses, vines and bushes, extending far beyond their rightful spaces, blocking the front walkway. After crossing their guard, my father switched on the seventies-style floor lamp abandoned by the previous owners and illuminated a room of my own, complete with pink striped wallpaper and a window offering a glimpse of the night sky.

I remember very little before Holliston, of our previous home in Uxbridge, of the walls that surrounded me as I spoke my first words and practiced my first steps, but I drove by decades later to show my young sons. While staring directly at my first home, the tiny, rickety structure on Kennedy Lane, my children asked me why there was no house next to the garage, and pieces of old stories started to fit together as simply as my children's puzzles.

We shared that house with three pets.

Brendan Behan, the attack cat, always resented my existence. He guarded his spot on my mother's lap with his sharp claws and long fangs. Legend has it that he sat on the roof, perched to jump on intruders, or guests, as they entered the front door, and that he once dragged home a dead woodchuck, with a scratch above his eye as his only collateral damage. I despised that cat.

Ed, the green canary, lived in the kitchen, basking in constant attention, as no corner of the house was far enough to provide respite from his incessant squawks. He died shortly after the move to Holliston, apparently succumbing to starvation when he was forgotten in a far away corner of the lower level of the split. As I recall, my only reaction to his passing was the humor I found in the rhyme of the news: Ed is dead.

Clementine, our ugly black and white hound, was a constant companion in the stories of Uxbridge: following me to the neighbor's house, where I was free to play with the older kids, accompanying us to the park alongside my brother's stroller, even jumping into the open door of the passerby's car who had hit the dog as he chased a squirrel across the street, as if ordering the driver to bring him to the vet. He was successful in that effort and he recovered promptly. The walls and postage stamp lot in Uxbridge were ultimately deemed too small for him, and my father eventually brought him to a farm that would provide him with room to roam. To this day both my parents maintain that they actually brought him to a farm, that the story was not a tale invented for the benefit of small children.

I guess I didn't fit in the space offered by our first home for long either.

Before I was one year old, I would gleefully crawl to my room when I was scolded. One early photograph from Uxbridge shows me, on my hands and knees, already a master of my space. With a smile embellishing my face, eternally-optimistic hazel eyes peeked out of my room to ask if my punishment was complete.

As soon as I could walk I began bouncing off the walls. I would walk into closed doors, ricochet off walls, and use the solid end of the hall to assist me in turning into the bedroom my brother and I shared. The familiar thud of my misestimation of space and time became so commonplace that my parents ceased to hear it. Guests would inquire, though, and I suppose they found it odd. For some reason it surprised neither me nor my parents.

We moved to Holliston on Halloween, and I trick-or-treated as a bunny with a puffy tail attached to my fuzzy footed pajamas at my grandparent's Hopedale house along the way. We had leapfrogged over their home for now, moving from five miles west of them along Route 16 to eight miles east. Both stops along the journey of a seemingly perpetual return to Hopedale.

Chapter 3
WHAT'S GOD GOT TO DO WITH IT?

(John, 4 years old)

1950: The Korean War begins; U.S. sends military advisors to assist South Vietnam; labor unions enjoy a rapid rise in membership, peaking in 1954.

Families like mine didn't buy houses. We rented space in them until the landlord found out there were six kids and we were asked to leave.

But not this time.

A loan of $6,000 from a local loan officer he had known since boyhood and had once protected from a couple homosexual-hating tough guys, let my shoe shop bed-lasting father buy a house from friends in his hometown. Rumor had it he was better friends with the wife than the husband, but we had a home. The four rooms were intended to house his family of eight soon to be nine.

We moved in October of 1950 to the place that I would call home for the rest of my life, although I only lived there until I was ten.

The driveway cut into the woods at 197 Purchase Street. It had been a long ride from Worcester. Now my uncle's 40s vintage black sedan followed the stone wall and crunched down the gravel drive to the front of the house.

It was tiny, even to a four-year-old. Its roof was bowed, the cedar shingles cracked, the furnace was falling apart, the sun porch clung to the side of the house by a few overmatched spikes, and half of the barn had already fallen down. It should have been condemned. It was to be our home. Maybe in a way it was condemned.

I was carried inside, out of the wind of the fall day, by a sister in powder-blue pedal-pushers, a white sleeveless blouse, and blond banana curls, and set on the counter in the kitchen pantry as she nearly ran away from the screaming. Truth be told, she probably felt the same way, but by ten she had already learned to bury disappointment inside.

As a crew of relatives and family bustled back and forth like hired hands, carrying and plunking on the floor what belongings we had, I screamed, only stopping to catch my breath and to observe the place that I would come to love more than any place I would live from that day forward. The place where we would become a family.

Inside the front door was a 4 x 4 mud room with a closet and a worn out slab of linoleum that curled at the corners. From there we had stepped into the kitchen. Its floor climbed, not subtly, uphill to what would be called the pantry although it harbored an ice box, a kerosene stove, a steel sink and the counter I had been sat upon. The wood-slat floor leveled off into the living room. They erected the girls' mahogany four-poster there. Off the living room were my parents' bedroom and the Little Room, where I would be sleeping sometimes with my brother, sometimes with my sisters. The Little Room had space for little more than a full-sized bed. That's it, just the bed.

My family never did seem to figure out the perfect sleeping arrangements. I guess it had to do with who was getting along with whom at the time and who was growing breasts.

In summer, some got to sleep out on the sun porch. There were three beds for kids that were moved from room to room as the girls grew up.

We slept head to foot to head, covered with coats my mother would buy for twenty-five cents a box at auctions.

It wasn't more than a few days later that I woke up with twin sets of feet in my face, Nancy's on one side and Sheila's on the other side. I guess the baby was sleeping with my parents. It was how you learned you were no longer the baby in this house. I would never sleep with them again.

There was a washroom in the back and two rooms upstairs, but we didn't use them because of the smell.

The aging cess pool had no chance of handling a family of eight and was always full to overflowing. That meant flushing the toilet was out of the question until we could come up with enough money to get it emptied. We sort of had an indoor outhouse. That meant we didn't use the laundry room attached to the bathroom and didn't climb the stairs that led from there to the two upstairs unfinished rooms either if we could help it.

In summer, the smell was the worst, and we avoided being in the house at all if we could find a reason to be outside. When nature called, we answered it outside by using what God gave us - the woods behind the house became our kitchen, play room and toilet most of the days and summer nights. In the winter we just tried not to breathe while going to the bathroom. The use of the woods as an additional lavatory also taught us early on the usefulness of knowing the difference between an oak leaf and poison ivy.

We learned how to live pretty much outside in the mined-out granite quarries, the forest surrounding the house, and the random sunny patches of warm pine needles in the woods. But at least we owned our own home. According to my oldest sister, Patty, this meant we were at least not the poorest people in Milford.

It might have been considered a hardship by some, but it wasn't long before the sisters of St. Joseph, who were the teaching corp at St Mary's, taught us how to "offer it up for the souls in purgatory," so we did, and we ate whatever was put on our plate because we knew the poor people overseas, who were sustained by "the Bishops' Relief Fund" and the money we students gave to "the missions," survived with much less. By the time I was in the third grade I was giving my "milk money" to the missions and hoping that God was watching.

But, by the fourth grade, I seriously doubted that "those poor people overseas" had less than my family, even as a third-grader at St Mary's Grammar School.

The nuns started my religious training with, "Who made me? God made me" "I believe in God, the father almighty creator of …" I had to stop Sister Francis Anna and ask, "Don't we have one of those 'in a nutshell' things I can go by? You know, to make a long story short?" She knelt beside my desk. Nuns were always kneeling. She smiled and said, "Treat everyone the way you want to be treated, and love God, and you'll be all right." I went by that. It was easier and made more sense, except I was pretty sure everyone wasn't treating me the way they wanted to be treated, even the ones in church on Sunday. Hell, especially them.

It was about this time that I had a day that nearly made me a cripple for life. My sister Sheila had become bored with dressing her paper dolls and had decided I was a fair substitute. She had put a dress on me against my stunned protests, but then when the black and white Cushman bakery panel truck came, she left me and ran back through the house to see what my mother might buy. I sat outside on the stoop. Dejected, I walked over and sat on the rear bumper of the truck. Suddenly, the truck jumped and started up the driveway toward the road. The jolt bumped me from the edge and I fell to the dirt driveway. It would have been fine, except the dress I was wearing had caught on a trailer hitch at the back of the truck, and I was being dragged up the dirt and stone drive and onto the tarred road on my knees. I fought to get the cloth off the hitch, but it had torn into a hole near the hem and was now snugly attached to the silver and rust ball. It took me about a quarter mile to pull myself up to the bumper with my right hand and unhook the dress from the truck with the other. I rolled to the side of the road. Both knees were bloodied, nearly shaved flat by the asphalt. I stood and walked back toward my house embarrassed and bleeding.

A doctor came that afternoon and poured raw alcohol onto both knees and scrubbed them with a gauze patch, creating the pain by which I would from then on judge all pain. He did this nearly every day for a month. By the end of the month I started screaming when his big black Desoto rumbled down the driveway. He said if the infection took hold I would not walk again. I prayed. It didn't take hold. I walked. From there on I figured God was real.

The author of our home life was Sweet Genevieve. The daughter of a factory boss, she had been brought up with food and clothes in a warm house polishing the silver on Wednesday, at the edge of Hopedale, a neighboring town we all knew as a rich town.

She taught us the manners of the dinner table, the hierarchy of a family, and on summer afternoons she read us the classics. I listened, sitting against the trunk of a Maple tree in the front yard, and dreamed along with the chivalrous adventures of Ivanhoe, the undefeated Jonathan Ridd and Lorna Doone, the ingenuity of Tom Sawyer, the sad Tales of Roland, and the adventure of Treasure Island. At night we listened to country music on the stand-up Philco, said our prayers and went to bed.

At the center of this over-extended family was my father: a high-school hero, a heart-throb in town (he looked eerily like Gregory Peck), and a hard worker when he could drag himself out of his innate Irish-Catholic depression and work without the aid of alcohol.

At times he had a full-time day job in the shoe factory and a full-time night job in the foundry. Eventually they found out he was Irish and fired him from the foundry in Hopedale. After that, life seemed to get to him every Thursday when he collected his $40 paycheck at the shoe shop and would drink it into $25 that would have to buy groceries for the week and anything else that came up, like the mortgage.

As wonderful a person as he was when sober, he was a mean drunk, and liked to break things in the house that he would never fix, like the window in the front door when my mother locked him out one payday and he punched a hole in it, opened the door and shouted for my mother to bandage his hand. She had to tear up one of my jerseys to dress the wound.

By the age of six or seven I had learned to stash peanut butter or a box of Kix under my bed so I could hide when he got home. In the morning, in a guilt-laden stupor, he fixed the window by tacking the back of a Cornflakes box over it with a map of Treasure Island on it. I read it every time I went out, until it melted in the hurricane of '55.

And there were times it got physical. Not often, but sometimes the devil entered our home.

But at dinner when he was sober his gleaming Irish eyes captured us all in a web of stories.

He told of the Portuguese families moving into Milford, and how the shoe shops were "taking mighty advantage of them. … You know, Jocko, if you don't have the dough, re, mi, boy, you better go back where you came from … But they can't go home, Jocko." He looked down at my wide eyes and said "They are here to stay just like we were, and the Italians were, and now the shop is giving them a different rate (per case of shoes) and half the chits to put in their books. And they don't speak English, so they can't fight back … And Jocko, a man stands up for what is right. Woody told it true, we gotta stick to the Union or woe betide ya."

And so he did.

He and a few Irish friends took Guthrie's advice and helped organize a union at the shop so the Portuguese workers, along with the Italians and Irishers, would all get a fair wage.

And for his efforts he was blackballed.

And his family learned the price of integrity, and we learned the proper meaning of righteous hunger.

Chapter 4
NOT AFRAID OF CLOWNS

(Mandy, 3-5 years old)

1982: The Equal Rights Amendment fails ratification; Michael Jackson releases Thriller; *Leonid Brezhnev and Princess Grace die.*

I learned to read an analog clock when I was three years old. I rose before the sun every morning, and after failed attempts to force further slumber, my mother opted for a different tactic and taught me that I was not to wake anyone else until the big hand was on the twelve and the little hand was on the seven. The rest fell into place on my daily viewing of those hands inching mercilessly toward my goal.

Before I started kindergarten at four years old, I had already learned to fill the mornings by running my own restaurant. For my grand opening, I dug through the fridge for the biggest item I could find, dragged a hambone from a platter on the middle shelf, placed it into a frying pan on the only burner I could reach, and turned the dial on the stove until the incessant clicking produced fire. I watched the brilliant blue flame flicker for a moment, and beaming with pride, I returned to the fridge for a side dish. Most items inside were large and unwieldy, and having already selected my main, big dish, I wanted something smaller, so I pulled a silver can off the bottom shelf and closed the door. After failed attempts to open it, I left my bone to fry unsupervised and went to my parents' bedroom. The little hand had not yet approached the seven, but I thought maybe they'd make an exception to wake just long enough to help me open one can before returning to sleep. I sat gingerly on their bed, and in the sweetest voice I could muster, I solicited help.

"Mom, Dad, I can't open this," I said, handing over the can of beer.

Eyes opened slowly at first, and then sprung wide.

"Good!"

"What's that smell?"

"Breakfast," I answered through an enormous smile.

Both were out the door before I could stand up, and by the time I returned to the kitchen, my hambone was in the trash, the frying pan was in the sink, the beer was in the fridge, and my mother was opening every window in the house while my father was stealing the batteries from the smoke alarms.

My cooking improved quickly, and my parents encouraged me in my endeavors, under the sole condition that I refrained from lighting the stove until the little hand reached the seven in the future.

Each morning I rose with the birds and prepared my restaurant. Menus listed a cereal section, with a perpetually misspelled title and a list of every box in the house, a bread section for bagels, muffins and toast, a drink section based on available juices, coffee, tea, and milk, and a special section offering a new carefully selected dish from my Better Homes and Garden's Junior Cookbook each morning. Those specials were the items I hoped everyone would choose, and the ones I obediently prepared, but did not cook, until my parents were awake. They usually humored me and chose my item of the day, although often after much teasing on their part and coaxing on mine, and it was that humoring that led my father to once consume a plate of scrambled eggs into which I had added a full tablespoon of salt instead of a ¼ teaspoon. He ate every speck of food on that plate with a smile on his face, and thanked me for a delicious breakfast. I took one bite and spit it out.

Often, especially as the years passed, I rose too early even to prepare my restaurant, and on those mornings, I enjoyed the television. When I was in first grade, a show called "Yes, You Can," featuring various professional athletes and teams aired at 4:30 a.m., and it was one of my favorites. It was typically followed on Boston's TV-38 by *The Willy Whistle Show*, a local program reminiscent of *Bozo The Clown*, but Willy, also a clown, emitted a whistling sound through his words when he spoke. I loved Willy Whistle the best, and one morning during breakfast I told my mother about him.

"It's really the best show on television," I started.

"Why do you think so?" She asked.

"He knows all sorts of local Boston things to do, and he's really funny."

"There are a lot of funny shows."

"I really want to know if he always whistles when he talks, or if he just does it for the show."

"What do you think?" My mother never forced her opinions on me, and my father didn't believe that there was ever just one right answer. This time it may have worked against them.

"I think I'll have to meet him to ask him," I answered.

"Okay, honey," she replied. I'm not sure she was still listening.

"Okay?"

"Sure, if that's what you want to do."

That was all the permission I needed to write Willy a letter telling him I wanted to meet him, seal it into an envelope, address it to Willy Whistle, TV-38, Boston, MA, find a stamp in the top desk drawer, and put it in the mailbox with the flag up for it to go out the next day.

A few weeks later, Willy himself called my house and asked to talk to me. He did not whistle when he spoke to me, but he did invite me to come onto his show. I think when a grown man called the house asking for their five year old daughter, my parents started paying more attention, and they took it from there. It was decided that I would be allowed to go on the show, as long as I took my little brother with me, and the adults selected a date. I prepared for my television debut for weeks, and decided to perform "I'm a Little Teapot" on the air. I practiced and I practiced and I practiced some more, until my father got sick of watching me and showed me an alternate version:

"I'm a little teapot,

Short and stout.

Here is my handle.

Here is my ... other handle.

Oh no, I'm a sugar bowl!"

The day before going on the air, I practiced for my classmates in Mrs. White's first grade. I performed as a sugar bowl and the entire class, teacher included, roared with laughter. I was mortified, and went home furious with my father. I hadn't realized it was supposed to be a joke, and I was expecting applause, not laughter.

Meanwhile, Mike had no interest in appearing on television, he was only four, not yet in Kindergarten, and fairly reserved.

The next morning we drove to the studios in Boston for the filming of *The Willy Whistle Show*. The set was intimidating, but Willy was incredibly kind and patient. He asked what I wanted to perform, and I told him. I rose, and I delivered the correct version of "I'm a Little Teapot" as well as I could. I raced through my words and slurred them together. My voice shook, as it still does when I speak in front of large groups, and I fought tears, but I was determined to conquer my fears.

Mike sat silently in his seat. He had not prepared, and did not want to perform. When I finished, Willy asked Mike what he wanted to do. Without moving from his seat, he pulled an imaginary carrot from his pretend pocket, and said:

"Naaaawww, What's up doc?"

He sounded exactly like Bugs Bunny.

Everyone, including Willy, laughed. Mike, straight-faced, waited for the laughter to end, and, with the impeccable comic timing he still possesses, repeated his line.

"Naaaawww, What's up doc?"

The place broke into hysterics.

It was one of the best Willy Whistle episodes ever made, in my clearly unbiased opinion.

Determination and unflagging efforts help us grow, but spotlights have a way of finding only those who aren't looking for them.

Chapter 5

I ALWAYS OPTED TO
BE THE INDIANS

(John, 6 years old)

1952: The Indian Relocation Program begins moving American Indians to the cities to work in factories; because of DDT there were only two cases of malaria in the U.S. and many countries credited it with eradicating the disease entirely; Jonas Salk reveals his polio vaccine; An article on the front page of the July 28 edition of the **Washington Post** *reports that a flying saucer outran the U.S. jet trailing it.*

Within a few years of the move to Purchase Street, we were pretty much settled into a routine.

Scrapper Jack had landed a job with a Jewish shoe shop owner who felt a kinship with the Irish. "No one likes either of us," he had explained to my father.

For a while we ate better. On some Saturdays we even had chocolate milk, mixed, of course, half and half with less expensive white milk. Sundays were Mass and dinner at Grammy's house, and we even metamorphosed into a situation where the Thursday night drunken tirades just became another rite of passage, something to be expected, something to be endured. You set your limits, and as long as no one got seriously physically hurt it was livable.

For me, summer days were a childhood heaven spent in the woods with Spike, Danny, Peter Boy and Robbie fighting the Indian wars (I always opted to be the Indians) or cavorting with Davy Crockett and George, "Be sure you're right, and then go ahead," or warming in the DeBoer's cultivated berry rows with my first love, the red-haired, freckled and beautiful Linda Chalmers. There were the sounds of cicadas, crows, chickens and barking dogs and our woods which my grandmother said were "owned by God, and so they are safe." Above, was the boom of jets breaking the sound barrier in a perfectly blue sky. Some hot nights in mid-summer there was the sweet smell of DDT sprayed from an airplane or a helicopter. I loved the smell of DDT. It usually meant sometime soon some random uncle or a friend of my mother's would pick us up and we would all go to the Mendon Drive-in. Then one summer I was old enough for Little League, and my Catholic religion now included baseball among its sacraments.

Beginning in the fall, school became practice genuflecting on the hardwood floors of St. Mary's Grammar School, Baltimore Catechism, warm milk stored on the radiator, a bag lunch of a peanut butter sandwich and an apple, worrying that my dad was going to hell because of his language, and my incessant stupid questions.

"Sister, if Jesus died Friday night and left the cave Sunday morning, how is that three days?"

"Sister, if faith is believing things you can't prove, what is ignorance?"

"Sister, at the time of the anti-popes, did the people know the popes weren't infallible?"

"Sister, the commandment says 'Thou shalt not kill,' how come God told Joshua to destroy Jericho and kill everyone inside the walls?"

Then came the day when I did something wrong and Sister Miriam Patrice yanked me from the schoolyard with a "Woe betide you young Mr. Hourihan if you …"

At that point I interrupted her, saying something such as, "You no good, Goddamn son of a bitch, get your Goddamn hands off me or I'll beat you within an inch of your life," at the top of my lungs.

This did not set well with the good and noble nun. She didn't even ask where I'd learned it.

Now, here I guess I should tell you that I had, months before, fallen down a set of stairs and cracked all my baby teeth and they were now a set of black fangs, I had yanked out my eyebrows (all of them, and my mother had penciled in new ones), and I had glasses and a patch over one eye. I looked, I guess, as evil as I sounded.

She began dragging me up the sidewalk toward the church, and when I went home and told my mother what they did to me next she laughed out loud and said, "They exorcised you ..." Then as an afterthought she added, "I hope it worked." My mother had a great smile. It cured anything.

I wasn't sure then where my anger had come from, but I suspect now that it was the scourge of being torn away from my woods, autumn Maple leaves, my pet squirrel, my birds, Butch the cat, Sea Bee the dog, my climbing tree, raspberries, blueberries, blackberries, snow angels, snow forts, sledding, shoe skating, baseball, Saturday morning black and white cartoons on the new TV with the broken horizontal hold, and most importantly, the amazing thrill of just being alive and unencumbered in a world that made sense to me.

It was replaced with school, and since so little of that made sense, and curiosity had its weighty price, anger soon followed.

At four-and-a-half years old, after the kindergarten teacher had thrown away my apple because I was eating it at the wrong time, as if there is a wrong time to eat an apple in fall, I walked myself out of that damn school, breezed my way to the center of town to Jimmy's cab stand, where I gave the driver my address, "197 Purchase Street," and went home. I did this nearly every day for a week, until the cab owner got tired of making the drive without being paid, and my sister Patty was called out of her fifth-grade class and told to take me home. We'd try school again next fall.

Within a year, I learned the words "laid off" and "unemployment office." The concept of homework, and Sunday Mass, and genuflecting - knee all the way to the floor or you would get slapped in the head from behind by the nuns who were watching you "so very closely."

As work became a problem, my father's drinking became worse, and soon we didn't have enough to buy any but the most essential groceries.

My mother sent us in the mornings to pick the wild blackberries and rhubarb, and in the afternoon to collect dandelion leaves. There were eggs "on the cuff" from the DeBoer's chickens, and we grew corn, and pole beans, asparagus, beets and grapes. After my shoe worker father tried to kill a chicken with a butcher knife that we also used to cut linoleum, and the chicken bit him, hot dogs and Spam became our staple meat. And we became accustomed to bread, water and sugar sandwiches, and on more affluent days bread, butter and sugar.

My mother called it, "playing the cards you were dealt," but she did it in a voice that mimicked my father.

There were serious conversations at dinner time about the work farm where people like us went when we ran out of things to eat. It didn't sound like all that bad a deal to me, but Scrapper Jack smiled that proud Celtic smile and said, "Yeah, we're not doing that." And so we didn't.

Through it all, we became closer and closer as a family. Sharing is easier when you have so little to share, and empathy grew on you when you could see the sadness openly displayed on the sweat-streaked faces of the people you love.

Neil was born, and Dennis got sick. And at that time when you got bad asthma you either moved to the dry heat of the Arizona desert or you died. And at that time, and in our situation, family was self. You took care of family.

My father found work or borrowed money or both, and it was settled. My father, my sister Diane, Dennis and I would move to Phoenix. The others would come later, when he could get enough money. Except for Patty, the oldest, who would stay and finish high school living with my Uncle Jim and Aunt Adele. She was a senior and thought she might get a scholarship as the valedictorian, and it would be one less mouth to feed. People considered things like that in those days. Strangely enough, what they didn't consider was birth control.

Chapter 6
THE WORLD CAN WAIT

(Mandy, 7 years old)

1984: The Soviet Union withdraws from the Summer Olympics in the US and several Eastern bloc countries follow; Geraldine Ferraro becomes the first woman nominated for vice president by a major political party; Doug Flutie wins the Heisman Trophy; The Cosby Show *debuts on NBC.*

Black raspberry jam is perfection.

When I was seven years old, my parents decided it was time for my mother to return full time to the insurance industry. She had found much success there before we were born, and after dedicating several years to raising my brother and me, she would find even more success in the years to come. For a few months the bus deposited me home from the second grade at an empty house, with my key tied on a string around my neck and my little brother in tow. Each day, after entering the garage through its open back door, I would unlock the side entrance, earning our passage into the dining room, while the neighbors kept a distant eye on me and Mike. I lost my key frequently that year, and rather than admit it again, I once tried to pick our lock with a screwdriver. My parents came home, called the police, and reported an attempted break-in. The officer figured out what had happened, but he didn't squeal on me. My father eventually left his job in sales and took an entry-level job working nights at the newspaper.

That transition was a time of war in my house, marked by screaming matches all around. It is the beginning in my memory of the tension and fighting that defined home until I left for college.

While second grade opened my eyes to a stressful reality, the summer that followed created an escape from it. Since my dad worked nights, he became "Mr. Mom" at a time when stay-at-home dads did not exist. The summer after second grade belonged to me and my dad. We played Wiffle ball, soccer and tag. We climbed trees and built the most amazing fort in our inspiring maple that I could ever imagine. We taught the little girl from three doors down how to use an "Irish napkin." And then we watched in amusement as she proudly showed her polite, reserved Japanese mother how to use the entire inside of her arm to wipe her face at the dinner table. But mostly, we meandered through the lightly wooded land behind our house, pausing after each step to pick black raspberries. I could not have hoped for anything more, and I cherished every moment of it.

I loved that land, and although it could not have been more than a hundred yards deep, it constituted a wilderness in my eyes. Before I ever stepped foot beyond the first maple, those woods gave me my favorite swing the day my younger brother fled to the house to escape the wolves I suggested resided there. I was five years old, and as the birds sang their encouragement from my woods, that swing lifted me to my first solo flight. With my back to the house, I faced the trees as I pumped my legs until I reached a new height, first experiencing the point of momentary free fall on the way back from the peak of the swing's forward trajectory. Exhilarated, I gripped the chains, pushed every one of my forty-five pounds forward, and primed myself for one more return. Once I reached the end of my path, I yanked backward on the chains with all my might, flattening my not quite four foot frame. Just before I arrived at the top again, I released, and soared in the direction of the robin's call. From the edge of the woods, I listened to the bleating sheep and mooing cows from the nearby barn all summer, and I watched the squirrels frantically hoarding acorns through the fall. As snow covered the path, the woods created a new serenity for the neighborhood, and I enjoyed their silence. Soon enough I was eavesdropping once more on the birds as they announced the rebirth of the spring. I would stay outside all day, whenever the weather allowed, but I obediently observed only from the periphery, never crossing their threshold.

That summer with my dad allowed me my first real opportunity to explore the thin forest from the inside, to appreciate the beauty of its world. Each morning that summer, before the sun shone its full force down on us, we grabbed buckets and allowed the stately maple to usher us down a small path from the back of our yard. The tiny fruit, planted only by nature, grew freely in ample sunlight that shone through the trees. My dad and I walked together, occasionally chatting, but mainly yielding to the blackbirds and chickadees, and simply enjoying each other's company, as I sampled the sweet fruit and he filled his bucket. Before our arrival these plentiful bushes had fed only the birds. Their songs welcomed us to share in their happiness, and I wished I could travel as they did. I hoped to explore the world, to take it all in, and to share my song along the way.

By the heat of the summer we had collected more berries than we could possibly eat in cereal, snacks and pancakes, but I still woke up early each morning, grabbed my bucket, and headed for the woods. In order to allow our expeditions to continue, my dad learned to make jam. Before I knew it, the basement overflowed with jars of black raspberry jam. We gave jam to everyone we knew, and probably many people we didn't know. We ate black raspberry jam every day for what felt like an eternity. My tears flowed when we opened the final jar of jam. That summer had been perfect. The jam bestowed the sweet taste of its memory, and I was not prepared to let it go.

Chapter 7
THE BEST PLAN THAT DIDN'T WORK

(John, 10-11 years old)

1956 -1957: Rosa Parks refuses to give her bus seat to a white man, leading to the Montgomery Bus Boycott, initiated by Martin Luther King Jr.; The Lone Ranger movie is one of the first Made-For-TV movies created; Gunsmoke debuts on CBS-TV.

We had moved before, but this move was different.

I fully expected to see Indians and live on a black-and-white ranch, like in *Gunsmoke* or *Fury* or *The Lone Ranger*. And although my mother answered my question with, "Sure, maybe," I was wrong, and she was just being a mother who had more important things to worry about.

It was 1956, I was ten years old, and the family had lost our house to the bank, my brother Dennis was getting real sick and we were moving to Phoenix.

My mother would travel from Framingham, Massachusetts to Chicago with us by train, then my father, sister Diane, Dennis and myself would go on to Phoenix the only way we could really travel the United States, by Greyhound bus along Eisenhower's highways, side-by-side with all of those who couldn't afford the price of one of those "new-fangled jet airliner contraptions."

At an overheated city bus station somewhere south of Chicago but north of New Mexico, we had to switch buses. The passengers filed out the door, onto the sidewalk and followed each other, a single-file crowd, inside the station.

We made our way between tan cardboard-sided suitcases with darker trim, and paraded down the corridor created by rows of polished wooden benches filled with sleeping men and vigilant women with drooping eyelids. A herd of dehydrated humans were in search of something wet, driven by the long ride almost as cattle on a drive when they have just smelled water.

I didn't know it, had no earthly inkling, but in a few seconds I was about to make the first major decision of my young life. It would stay with me forever.

The line for the water fountain was long. There were women who had unashamedly hiked their skirts up; some even tucked them into their belt on one side. The streets outside were ninety degrees, and the air moving from the one stand-up fan near the information booth did little to combat the pre-heated oven inside the terminal.

In the front of the line was a big man in a light blue work shirt and tan pants. His belly rolled over his belt and hid it. As he bent over to drink, I saw that a large part of the center of the back of his shirt was drenched in sweat as if he had been piece-working, not riding an air-conditioned bus. He kept drinking and drinking until someone called him a camel, and Scrapper Jack, who was right behind me in line, laughed.

Then I noticed it.

There was a second fountain only thirty or so feet from the one that held the line hypnotized. This other fountain had no line of people.

I turned to my father. He had seen it too, but he didn't look as happy as I did.

"Look at the sign" he said.

Behind the new fountain was a white sign with black lettering that said "COLORED."

I turned back to the one at the end of the line I was standing in and it said "WHITE."

I was confused. I looked back for advice or at least an explanation.

I only knew two "colored" men in my short New England life: One was Buster who dropped off "homework" for my mother from the hat shop, and then picked up the finished hats a few days later. The other was Jackie Robinson.

I loved it when Buster drove his Lish Hat truck down the driveway. My mother always saved an orange soda for him, and we would sit on the back bumper of his truck and talk. He always shared his soda with me, so Buster was one of my favorite people in the world.

The second was Robinson.

My father and I always spoke in terms of baseball. When you have so little in your life you are naturally and magnetically drawn to the fairness of the national pastime. In every situation in baseball, in order for someone to fail, someone has to succeed.

He always told me to play like Jackie Robinson. He called him "fearless" and pointed out, "That man has intestinal fortitude," something that was life-and-death important to my old man. According to the Scrapper, 42 was someone to be emulated, so that was good enough for me.

But there was still the dilemma of the two fountains.

"It's your call, Jocko," he said, and put his hand on the back of my neck as he always did when we walked in certain parts of Milford. He was standing straight up like a rooster protecting chicks, and watching

31

the crowd that was now paying strange attention to us. The camel guy slowed down on his walk past us, and my father said, "Just keep moving." The big man did, but the rest still stared.

I was thirsty, very thirsty, but I knew if I drank from the "colored" fountain it would cause some problems the way we were being looked at, and I knew for sure I couldn't drink at a fountain where Buster and Jackie Robinson wouldn't be allowed.

I didn't drink from either. Instead I turned and walked off toward the door to the outside and the buses.

Scrapper Jack slapped me on the back like I had just hit a homerun. "Well," he said, "it looks like we ain't doing this." He added, "You gotta pee?" I looked up at him in question. "Yup, they got a sign there too." We laughed and left. I peed against the building next to the bus in full view of everyone sitting next to its windows. I figured anyone could do that.

I thought of what Woody said about this stuff. "Maybe if I hadn't seen so much hard feelings, I might not could have felt other people's."

A few days later we landed on the sidewalk in the dead-still heat outside the Greyhound station in the center of Phoenix, and I realized I was probably not going to be living with Indians or on a ranch.

It took me many more years to fully understand what had happened that day: that my father was ready and willing to take on that whole segregated bus station rather than let his kid grow up a racist. He treated everyone with respect until they gave him a reason not to, and if they were hating people for the color of their skin color it was apparently a good reason not to.

Ever since then, when I meet a racist I blame it on his parents.

But it was at that time that I began to fully understand that a man stands up for what is right, damn the consequences, that Phoenix is as hot as hell, and that people carried six-guns strapped to their hips.

After a few weeks sweltering in a dark brown hotel room with a broken floor fan, above the Greyhound station, Diane, 15, jet black hair, striking looks, and the hips, waist and chest of a 20-year-old, got a job at the bus station diner as a waitress. She got lots of tips. Scrapper Jack took a job as produce manager at a Bayless market uptown, I got my molar pulled after a couple nights of excruciating pain, and we moved to Second Avenue on a tip Scrapper Jack got from a guy in a bar.

There were six "apartments" in the old tin-sided, rounded-roof Quonset hut - three rooms each, on a slab of concrete bordered on the back side by an auto junkyard and the Silver Dollar Saloon, and on the front side by an irrigation ditch followed by a fence and then the desert.

I loved the desert. It was warm, quiet and comfortable.

Also in the Quonset there were the Texans, Lonnie and Garland; the Ardenhursts, Tom and Tic from Tennessee, and Max Wood. My father was called Boston, and I was Li'l Boston, and everyone just stared at Diane like a thirsty man stares at water in a desert.

We didn't know it, but all of us people in that row of "apartments" were considered white trash stuck in the middle of a barrio. The Mexicans looked down on us. We were all poor, but at least it was their country. It seemed no one in Phoenix was born here except the Mexicans.

We didn't even know the word barrio, but the rest of Phoenix did, and they also knew the meaning of the words white trash.

It was the family down beyond the Tennessee Ardenhursts' that became a problem for me.

It was only a number of weeks after we landed in this foreign country that I was walking along the back side between the Quonset and the fence to the junkyard, teasing the guard dog across the fence, when a kid I had never seen before charged out the back door of the apartment where he was apparently visiting, wielding a steak knife.

He took a swing at my face and missed. He outweighed me by quite a bit, but it never occurred to me that I would lose this fight. The only fight I had ever lost was in third-grade and that was to a giant. I stepped inside his next lunge and grabbed his arm, stepped under it, pulled it behind him, shoved it up his back and told him I'd break it if he didn't drop the knife. I felt like Cheyenne Brodie. He dropped it. I picked it up and threw it to the dog, who dutifully picked it up and ran off.

Weaponless now, he ran inside, but by the time I got to the front of the Quonset, he was being shoved out the front door by an adult I figured was his old man who was telling him, "Kill that Yankee son of a bitch."

We fought for a while with everyone from the neighborhood watching. It was a one-sided affair. He was too slow to hit me, but I was too small to really hurt him punching him in his fat gut. Finally Nancy said in utter frustration, "Oh for God sake Johnny, hit him in the face." I did, and he ran inside crying, where he got beat up by his jerk of an old man. That's where I got my reputation and a fist full of friends, and more than a few looks by one of the Ardenhurst girls.

The Texans, the red necks from Tennessee, and my brother Dennis and I became our own posse.

We played marbles and fought with some of the Mexicans. I guess they didn't like us. We played yo-yos and kites and cards and dice and baseball and knife throwing. We gigged frogs and caught fish to eat, and we made money by coaxing scorpions into the neck of coke bottles with a short piece of stick, covering it with a bottle top with holes in it and selling them to people who wanted a scorpion but had enough brains not to get them by coaxing them into a coke bottle with a short stick.

It made money quicker than altering the pay telephones on street corners to hold their coin-return until the end of the day when we would reach our skinny fingers up inside the slot and pull out the wad of paper and collect the change. Sometimes we would unplug the soda machine in front of Bayless, then plug it in at the end of the day and hit the coin return, or we would steal deposit bottles out the back of the Safeway where they were stored and return them in the front.

It wasn't a lot of money, but we all got to eat and buy stuff we needed, like underwear, baseball cards and cigarettes.

I attended Rio Vista School where most everyone spoke Spanish, but strangely I found that no one in my grade saw me as different. I was a fast runner, a fair fighter, an all-star pitcher, someone you could count on to stand up when needed, a Catholic like them, and that's who I was to most them. To me they were just people from Arizona. Later, when we began picking cotton to make some grocery money, not all of them were even from Arizona. I think they were from Mexico.

The wind off the southern desert did nothing to cool the day, and as a pre-teen living in the endless heat of the barrio, I was bound to have a short stint on the bad side of the law. The first thing I learned is it is better to be the brains of the outfit than it is to be the other end.

Scrapper Jack himself was proud of his boy (me) the night everyone else's kids were arrested for a shoplifting endeavor that the store manager said was "the best thought-out plan" he had "ever seen not work."

But that's getting ahead of the story.

Myself and the Texans and the Ardenhursts and Max would meet at the junkyard every few days, pester the pit bull, and go to the supermarket across the big street to steal candy and stuff.

I loved walking out into the oncoming traffic and timing the passing cars so I could sidle right up a few inches from the side door as they passed then dart between the trunk and the hood of the next car as I crossed. I liked the feel of the wind, I suppose.

Inside the door of the market, to the left, was a line of registers and the main store. To the right, was the candy row. Perpendicular to others, it was wedged between the front plate-glass window and the courtesy booth, and was pretty much untouchable, but there were some candy bars in the general part of the store too. The really big adult–sized Hershey bars were up the center aisle, so every few days we would grab one or two of those stuff them in our pants, skirt the cash registers, and speed out the door.

We never got caught, but I saw a problem. And, as I told them all after a game of kick-the-can one particularly cool and breezy night, "It's just not a challenge."

I explained my plan. "We go inside the front door as a group." I stopped for effect, like the bad guys on TV.

"Everyone but you two Ardenhurst boys. You two wait outside.

"Then, go in arguing and go right in front of the registers so everyone sees you. You gotta make it believable."

"Then Tommy here whacks you in the mouth in the pickle aisle."

"What?" Tic is unsure of this plan.

"Remember when those two redneck kids had a fight the other day? Think about what happened."

The courtesy booth had emptied. The cashiers all ran down to stop the fight, and the manager went with them because they were in the pickle aisle. That could get messy if the jars started breaking, and no one wanted to clean that up.

I told them how the rest of us would just hang around in front by the inside Dr Pepper machine.

"Then you two start wailing on each other."

This was no problem since the two cousins were always wailing on each other for one thing or another. I attributed it to them being brought up in the hills of Tennessee before the whole family rustled themselves out to Phoenix.

"Then when everyone goes running to the fight, we fill up our shirts and just run like hell

out the front door big as life. What do you think?"

"Sounds great" Tommy said, "When do we do it?"

"Tomorrow afternoon."

Well, Coach Lyons called an unscheduled baseball practice because we had to get ready for the playoffs, and I forgot all about the plan.

My team practiced until dusk, and I came home to a darkened house.

All the parents and all the kids were at the Texans'. I looked in the window and it didn't look promising. Someone saw me and called me inside.

Tex, the boys' father, was doing the parental honors.

Tex was big, 6-5 or so, and wide, and he wore boots and a cowboy hat. I could never for the life of me figure out if he was a good guy or a bad guy.

"Y'all done a bad thing, heah. You jes don't steal stuff. It ain't right. And ya don't get caught cuz that's jes stupid." I looked at Garland, the older

Texan boy, who wagged his head to shut me up. I knew he wouldn't tell because kids like us didn't rat on our friends.

"Now, the po-lice say they'll leave this to us, but we gonna have ta punish all y'all."

"No fishing. No candy. No TV. No baseball."

"No baseball?" Max and I were the only ones on the team. The playoffs were just starting and we could end up in the Little League World Series. This was too much punishment.

"Not you Li'l Boston. You ain't gonna be punished. You wasn't theah."

My father put his arm around my shoulder and said, "Well, don't be too hard on them Tex. C'mon Johnny let's go home."

As he was telling me over the kitchen table how proud he was when the cops called and then brought the whole passel of kids home and I wasn't there, my mother raised an eyebrow smiled and shook her head.

I learned something else that night, about being on the wrong side of the law, and I told the others the next day.

"It ain't my fault. You all should know better than to go along with a plan that ends 'and then run like hell.'"

The moral of the story is organized sports keep kids out of trouble.

I can vouch for that.

By the time the South Mountain High School coach was talking to Scrapper Jack about where I would be playing baseball next season, and I was thinking of how I could steal a motor scooter, and I had to deal with my sister becoming my mother, my real mother, Neil and the twins, Nancy and Sheila, arrived. It wasn't long before she said, "We ain't doing this anymore," and we up and moved back east.

We made the move the same way we had arrived - in shifts. My dad, Dennis and the twins stayed behind living in a trailer with a broken toilet. I was told they had to go to the landlord's house and ask to use the toilet. Sometimes they were told, No. It's a good thing we had all learned at an early age how to handle that situation.

My old friends back in Milford were still the same, but I wasn't.

I had become someone who was filled with the anger that had begun with the move from Worcester and built through my father's ordeals and demons that so directly flowed downhill to the rest of us, to the few years of knife fights and fist fights and a lot of running away in a barrio next to a junkyard with a pit bull that I liked to piss off, and now I was back where I had started. My life floated along in a red cloud as I tried to fit back into the comfortable childhood innocence at St. Mary's school protected by God, my family, and a circle of friends whom I no longer knew or, rather, who no longer knew me.

Chapter 8
HOME AGAIN, HOME AGAIN

(Mandy, 9 years old)

1986: The Challenger explodes; a nuclear accident at Chernobyl alarms the world; the New England Patriots get destroyed by the Chicago Bears in Super Bowl XX; "We Are the World" wins song of the year.

I was nine years old and my brother was eight when we left our home. My mother was always looking at new houses that we could not afford, but I had not realized she had seriously considered moving. Even as we embarked on the half-hour drive for our weekly visit to my grandparents' house, I suspected nothing. While I devoured salami sandwiches and chatted with my Italian grandmother, I noticed my grandfather milling around the house. Papa spent most of his time in the garden, chasing snakes from the cucumbers with a small shovel. He usually only entered the kitchen in an attempt to regale us with a tomato larger than the one he had picked the previous week. This week something was different. My normally reserved, jovial grandfather seemed to have something up his sleeve. I started to become more aware of the content of my conversation with my grandmother. It was different from normal. She was telling me all about Hopedale: how the people were nicer, the schools were better, and the soccer was more competitive. In the middle of the afternoon, my grandfather told us to get in the car. It did not occur to me to ask him why. He drove us about half a mile up the hill to "Pinecrest," a brand new development in Hopedale, and my parents bought a house.

Two months later we moved into the brand new house. By the end of the school year, I had learned a lot about Hopedale: that the people were not nicer, the schools were not better, and the soccer stunk. We spent most of our first summer in the house alone together, exploring our new surroundings.

The frogs seemed to own the backyard. Although they lived amidst the algae in the runoff pond, down the rocky cliff behind the house, I fell asleep to their banter every night. Since the yard had not yet been landscaped, the driveway stood at least 3 inches above the dirt. My brother and I spent the beginning of our first summer there playing "horse" or one-on-one on the makeshift basketball court in the driveway. Every third or fourth shot that went in would ricochet off the edge of the pavement and head down the gentle slope of the side yard. If Mike or I didn't catch it in time, the ball would eventually launch over the edge of the cliff, and dart down to the banks of the frog's pond.

One day by the time Mike and I scrambled down the cliff, the ball had reached the middle of the pond. Since neither of us particularly wanted to wade through the thick, slimy water, and neither of us would admit the cause of our hesitation, only one solution was possible. We abandoned the runaway basketball and invented a new game. We had not yet closely examined at the pond. The frogs, so loud at night, were serenely silent that afternoon. Based on the depth of their voices, we had assumed these frogs were at least the size of a baseball, but we were wrong. Mike spotted one first and pointed it out to me. The golf ball sized creature blended right in with the mucky pond. As I examined his frog more closely I saw another, and another, and another. There must have been thousands of frogs in this tiny pond. Mike reached into the brown water and grabbed one. While he was still investigating his prize, I caught one of my own. Then I looked at my frog, and at Mike's, and I realized his was bigger than mine, so I fished out a second frog. "Now I have two and you only have one" I thought; or did I say it? From there developed our new sport: frog-catching.

For the next few weeks, we spent the better part of each day competing over the frogs. "Look at this one!" "This one's browner," or "greener" or "more speckled than yours!" The frogs didn't seem to mind. We listened to their croaks every night, yet they were silent all day long. I assumed that if our game was upsetting them, they would have told us. One day Mike escalated the game by bringing a bucket to the pond. When I inquired as to the purpose of the bucket, his critical glare instructed me that although I desperately wanted to know the answer, I couldn't ask again. As the day went on, and I continued my usual exclamations about how my frog was bigger or more special than his, Mike collected frogs in his bucket. By the time I discovered the new rules of the game he had already won. At the end of the day Mike proclaimed his victory, and dumped his frogs back into their pond.

Bucket in-hand, I eased my way down the cliff through the blinding glare of the next rising sun. All day I collected frogs. I was careful to keep water in the bucket so as not to upset them. Mike joined me at some point, but didn't stay long. At the end of the day I brought my bucket back up the cliff to show my little brother that I had beaten him at his own game. By the time I showed Mike, my parents called us to dinner. I carefully stationed my bucket of frogs on the table on the back porch, so that the dog could not reach them, and went inside to clean up for dinner.

As I listened to the cries of the frogs that night, I realized I had forgotten to return my prize to their home. I thought about dragging my sleepy body out of bed, scrambling down the rocks, and touching that thick water in the dead of the night to return my friends to safety. But I was afraid, so I didn't. I tried to fall asleep. Whenever my eyes shut, I dreamt that my bed was full of basketball-sized frogs with fangs. Every time I awoke I heard their cries from the back porch. When the first hints of morning bled through my window, I rushed down to the back porch to save the frogs, but my bucket was empty.

When I wandered down the cliff that morning, I found Mike at the pond catching frogs, blissfully unaware that anything had happened. My frog-catching days were over, but I couldn't admit I was quitting, and I certainly couldn't tell him I was afraid of The Attack of the Giant Fanged Frogs. Instinctively, I walked to the pond beside him, reached into the water, grabbed a handful of green slime from the surface, and threw it right at him. In a sudden panic I turned and sprinted into the woods. We were off.

We had not yet explored the enticing forest behind the pond. My parents stayed out of the woods. My mom preferred to sit on the porch with a book, and my dad said he spent enough time in the woods in Vietnam to last a lifetime. When I sprinted into the trees that day, I found a whole new world. Mike was chasing me, algae in hand, so my first experience was a bit of a blur. As I raced around the trees, stumbled through the streams and scampered over the stonewalls, my only coherent thought was escaping from my brother. I couldn't see him, but I knew he couldn't be far behind. I was a faster runner than he, but he had better balance. I knew that he would emerge from the maze of wildlife and stones at any second. I kept running.

Before long, I too was wearing a splotch of green algae on my tee shirt. As much as I hated being caught by my little brother, I felt a strange feeling of relief at that moment. The chase was over, and there was a great forest to explore. With the competition behind us, Mike and I wandered through the woods together all afternoon. Most New England stone walls were old property lines, created by European settlers as a way to rid their land of rocks, as well as to denote the borders. As we navigated amongst the walls, I explained their history to Mike. To my surprise, he seemed interested. We followed one of the walls to the far edge of the woods, and we emerged in the town cemetery. I wondered briefly if the frogs were there, firmly shook the thought from my head, and declared that we shouldn't play in the cemetery. We returned to explore more of the woods.

No more than a few hundred yards back into the woods from the cemetery we discovered two big square holes. About 25 feet square and enveloped by thick vines, we almost stumbled into them without noticing that they extended a few feet into the ground. As we peered into the holes, I looked up and noticed the stonewall we had been following. Swiveling in place, I was fascinated to see that the stonewall encircled us. We had discovered the foundations of someone's home. The stonewalls were so much more beautiful and dignified than the orange plastic flags tied to the top of three foot stakes that marked the corners of our current property. I looked for my brother, who was sitting on the stonewall, peaceful.

We sat there for a short time soaking in the place. I wondered who had lived there, what the houses had looked like, and why this was all that remained. I wondered if one person or a whole family had pushed those stones off the property and piled them into a wall, and how they managed to stack them so well that they were still in place today. I wondered how long ago all that happened.

At dinner that night we told our parents about our adventure. My mother was far more interested in the dirt holes than we expected. After dinner, my grandmother appeared at the house. Since she rarely left her kitchen other than nightly bingo excursions, it was a wonderful treat to have a chance to give her a tour. I eagerly tried to show her my bedroom. To my surprise, my aging grandmother told me that she wanted to see the holes we had found. I was a bit skeptical of taking a woman who moved slowly in those days into the woods, as it was starting to get dark.

"Gram, can we go tomorrow instead?" I asked her.

"I'm here now," she replied.

So I helped her down the rocky cliff, past the chirping frogs, and into the woods. To my surprise, my grandmother was far more agile and at home in the woods than I had expected. She descended the cliff slowly,

but once we passed the pond, I struggled to avoid the embarrassment of falling behind her.

Although she had asked me to lead her, she seemed to know where we were going. When we reached the stonewall, my grandmother stopped, sat down, and smiled. Her eyes brightened until they overshadowed her wrinkled face.

"This was my first home," she explained to me.

The two of us climbed over the small wall together, and approached the foundations. She answered all the questions I had idly wondered about that afternoon. My grandmother seemed so proud and content to be able to share her childhood home with me, and somehow that conversation finally helped me feel that my new house could become my home. That night, as I fell asleep to the melodies of the frogs, I wondered if my grandmother had listened to those frogs all those years ago.

Chapter 9
HEREDITY VS. ENVIRONMENT

(John, 11 years old)

1957: Jackie Robinson retires from baseball rather than being traded; Wham-O creates the first flying disc; the Soviet Union launches Sputnik; the first rocket with a nuclear warhead is tested in Nevada.

The wind-driven rain on Main Street in Milford on the day of our return from Arizona was different from the surprise rain storms that ended the Phoenix dry season.

In Phoenix, when it rained, we played. People were happy.

So the 11-year-old running through the ever-filling puddles on the sidewalks of Milford, his T-shirt and cut-off jean shorts soaked, and stopping every few store fronts to open his mouth and look up at the sky like some demented turkey committing suicide was something to be stared at by the local women and children shoppers huddled under awnings along the route to Kennedy's butter and egg store.

In Milford, my hometown, when it rained people hid in doorways, hustled by under umbrellas or just stayed indoors until it stopped.

I was happy to be home, but, from the looks I was getting from those I puddle-jumped past, I was not sure they were going to be happy to have me. Although this was my natural habitat, in the wilder southwest where we had migrated, I had evolved.

book in your hand would elicit all the respect needed to go unquestioned through a store as you filled the bag with playing cards, jack knives, books, airplane models, CO_2 cartridges for Bugs' pellet gun, and whatever else I wanted but couldn't buy. Once I tucked a rotisserie chicken under my coat and walked right out through the front door of McCausland's with the confidence of a cat in a box of Easter chicks. I was hungry, and there wasn't anyone else going to feed me. We did this nearly every afternoon just after school let out for the day so it would look normal for us to be in the toy departments of Woolworth's or Grant's or the aisles of The First National supermarket. No one ever asked to see what was in the bag. They just smiled at the cute little Catholic boys.

One afternoon I marveled over the fish tank full of goldfish and guppies at Woolworth's, and I devised a great plan to use as a diversion so Bugs could grab a handful of View Master discs undetected. At home, I used a potato peeler to slice a piece of carrot a few inches long and thin enough to almost see through. I cupped it in my hand until I was at the tank and the woman sales clerk was nearby. I plunged my hand into the tank, pulled it out with a splash and wiggling the carrot, stuffed what appeared to be a goldfish into my mouth and swallowed. The clerk went ballistic, and while she was ushering me to the front of the store, Bugs could have taken all the discs in the display without being seen, if he hadn't been laughing so damn hard.

In the seventh and eighth grades the nuns gave me a break. All they saw was the prodigal son who had returned to the hallowed halls of St. Mary's grammar school, freckle faced, cowlick in the back, smiling and saying politely, "Excuse me sister," as I walked by, or nodding my head with great reverence every time they said "Jesus."

They didn't see the kid who would spend his lunch hour sneaking out of the school yard and going to the Italian penny candy store down the street to steal candy.

Life was good. I knew what I could take and what I couldn't take, and who I could take and who I couldn't take, and I knew how to keep what I was doing from my parents, the police and the school. And I had a way to come out even with the rest of the kids my age.

My only problem now was confession.

"Bless me father for I confess to almighty God, and to you father that I have sinned ..." I had to go to confession every week, since I didn't want to go to hell.

I smoked Pall Malls and drank Ruppert Knickabocker beer; I snuck into the movies and went to carnivals, fireworks and baseball games to hang out and cause trouble. I travelled with friends who did the same. And no one but a few close friends had any idea what my life was really like.

One afternoon when I was particularly thirsty, I even utilized my sister Nancy. We were close enough in age so that when we went into Carmichael's Drug Store and sat at the soda fountain and ordered a "Special" (a five cent glass of orange Zarex) and then asked for two straws, the guy behind the counter, who had no idea we were related, would keep filling the glass just to watch us because we were, "so cute." We drank about a gallon of the stuff, and then he wouldn't even take the nickel.

I never thought anything I was doing was being done for any reason other than necessity. I had, somewhere in the southwestern desert, decided I was tired of not having what other kids had. I intended to work for it when I was old enough. I even took a run at a morning paper route but got ripped off by the guy who was collecting the money. I saw it as a sign from God. So I figured I would wait for a real job, but right now I figured I would just take what I needed. Things were going pretty well, but then, in the middle of the ninth grade we moved again.

This time to Hopedale, a town run by Draper Corp., said to be the largest manufacturer of looms in the nation, a factory where my Scottish maternal grandfather had been a boss, and where my father wasn't allowed to work because he was Irish. And it seemed its school was in the business of manufacturing workers for the factory.

The town we were moving to didn't show a great appreciation for Catholics or Jews, it didn't seem to like Irish or outsiders of any sort except that they could be used as workers. There were absolutely no black people, or brown or Asian, and as much as the genetics of this lily white Protestant town didn't like any of these groups, it just flat out hated people from Milford.

My life was about to start getting very interesting.

Chapter 10

SOMETIMES THERE IS NO GRAY AREA: IT'S JUST BLACK OR WHITE

(Mandy, 11 years old))

1987: Iraq fires missiles at the USS Stark; Oliver North admits lying to Congress and shredding documents in an effort to aid the Contras; the U.S. Supreme Court rules that the Rotary Club must admit women.

It wasn't long before Mr. Wallace's classroom interrupted my summer adventures. My final year in elementary school was the rockiest year of my formal education and the only time in my life when I have not enjoyed being a student. I had never been in trouble in school before or after, but I was reprimanded every day that year. My first offences were minor: I slouched. Yes, this was a public school in the 1980s, and I was regularly punished for slouching in my chair. My teacher questioned everything I did and seemed to expect me to fail. If eraser marks marred my homework, he accused me of cheating and changing answers after I got to school, and on the one occasion when I honestly left my homework on the living room couch, he called me a liar.

For the most part, I kept my mouth shut and accepted his criticism, until one day when we discussed the impending presidential election. It was the fall of 1987, and candidates were just beginning to emerge. In an effort to educate us about the major candidates, Mr. Wallace split the room in half. He assigned one half Governor Dukakis and the other half Vice President Bush, and he instructed us to gather information about our candidate and prepare for a debate. The assignment sounded like one I would enjoy, and after his instructions I patiently raised my hand and waited for him to call on me.

"Which side has Jesse Jackson?"

"Neither side. Weren't you listening?"

"I was, but I thought I missed something. Do you want me to research Jesse Jackson on my own? I don't mind."

"No. You're assigned Michael Dukakis. We're only considering major candidates for this project."

I know now that I should have stopped there and accepted my teacher's assigned role, but for some reason, I didn't. And honestly, I wasn't trying to antagonize him. I was genuinely confused. The primaries had not yet happened, and I was aware that Jesse Jackson was in the primary. I assumed that since I was aware of him, he must count as a major candidate.

"But Jesse Jackson is a major candidate. I saw it on TV." I had also overheard my parents discussing his candidacy in a way that made me think they may consider voting for him.

"That's enough! You have been told your assignment, stop wasting our time."

With that, I shut up, but I couldn't get it out of my mind. I'm pretty sure he didn't, either.

My anger had grown by the time I arrived at my grandparents' house that afternoon. I recounted the story to my grandmother. She consoled me, but agreed with my teacher. "He's right," she told me directly. "He can never win."

"Why not?"

"Well, honey, I'm all for that civil rights and all, but he's black. We can't have a black president."

This sparked my first and only real argument with my grandmother. It lasted for almost two hours, until my mother stopped by on her way home from work to collect me. When I pleaded my case to her, she told me in no uncertain terms that she agreed with me, and that I was not to argue with my grandmother.

For the next few weeks I visited my grandmother only sporadically. I loved her, and relished my daily visits with her, but this marked my first exposure to racism, and it took a form I had never considered. It came from both my teacher and my grandmother, and was less direct than I had read about in history classes. At home alone after school, I was bored. One evening I whined to my parents about my boredom, and they suggested I think of something to do. I glared back, and my mother caved and offered a suggestion.

"Why don't you start a petition?"

"About what?"

"Anything."

"Huh?"

"What is something you don't like and you want to improve."

"I don't know, school lunch?" I asked, sarcastically.

"Sure. Start a petition for better school lunches."

I took the suggestion literally, went upstairs, and designed a petition. At bedtime I asked what to do with it, and my parents told me I had to collect signatures. I thought that would be simple, since no kid likes school lunch, so I brought it to school with me the next day.

The first day was easier than I had expected. I had a substitute teacher, so passing it around my classroom was easy. At recess I collected signatures from the other fifth and sixth graders. Then I passed it to my brother in the hallway and he targeted the third and fourth graders at their recess. I had lunch with the second graders, and half the first graders couldn't read, so I completed my day there.

The next day Mr. Wallace returned. He saw my petition on my desk and confiscated it. He walked silently to the front of the classroom, read it to himself, and placed it on his desk. I asked when I could have it back, and he told me that was the principal's decision. I was mortified. I slouched into my desk, struggling to hide my tears. By the end of school that day, my petition had been torn to pieces.

Days passed before my parents asked if anything ever came from my petition. I initially avoided the question, assuming I had done something wrong, and hoping to avoid punishment or worse, admitting my failure. My father saw right through me, and his questions would not relent until I succumbed and told them the whole story. My dad's face grew red with anger at his little girl's troubles, but it was my mother who spoke first, calmly.

"That's against the law."

The next morning my mother visited the principal, and by lunch everyone in the school had apologized to me. My father worked for the newspaper, so they got involved, too. Before I knew it I was on the front page of two separate newspapers as a crusader for better school lunches. When interviewers asked what I specifically wanted to see happen, I had no answer, so I said whatever came to my mind first.

"We need fluffernutters as an option instead of just PB&J."

Brilliant.

We did get more than that, though. I presented to the school committee, and they created a task force with representatives of each grade, administration, and the cafeteria manager. It turned out that the cafeteria workers had been trying to improve lunches for a while, so this gave them the impetus to make real, lasting changes.

I don't think Mr. Wallace forgot that incident, either.

As the year progressed, my reading scores declined. Our language arts curriculum consisted almost exclusively of a speed reader program. In small groups, by reading level, we sat in a corner, read a passage projected onto a screen, and answered questions. At the lowest levels, we were given the text to dissect one paragraph at a time, and we could refer back to the passage while answering questions. With each increase in reading levels, smaller amounts of text would be illuminated at a time. First we were reduced to three lines of text at once, then two, then one, and at each step the increment would be displayed for shorter intervals. Once you reached the highest levels, the light would move across one line, with progressive speeds, until at the peak level you could not even see an entire word at a time. It was a nightmare for me, and I was sure I was the only student moving backwards in the program. I could just never figure out how to answer the questions correctly at the end. In April we took the Iowa Tests of Basic Skills, and my score revealed a reading level of 4.8. I was in the sixth grade and knew enough to realize that placed my abilities at the fourth grade level.

So I did what any kid who thought she was smart until she read otherwise would do; I shredded the paper, until it matched my petition, until the pieces were small enough to stuff down the storm drain. Then I lied to my mother, telling her I never received my test results.

Outside of school I thrived. Once my petition excitement waned, I developed into an entrepreneur. I started my own babysitting club and distributed flyers throughout the neighborhood. No one hired me when

I was eleven, but I did start getting calls in the next year or two. When that didn't prove immediately lucrative, I started a kid's newspaper for the neighborhood. We only produced one issue, but it was a good one. I planned a field day for the little kids and even made awards and bought medals. Unfortunately, it rained on the scheduled day and no one showed up at the park. My most successful endeavor was my franchised lemonade stands. I set up lemonade stands at several corners around the development, and convinced friends to sit at each stand while I biked between them, collecting money as I went. Even in a franchised fashion, lemonade stands don't make much money, so eventually I gave up and got a paper route, which my brother and I kept, with the help of parents and grandparents, for several years.

As school came to a close I could not have been more excited to escape Mr. Wallace and what I believed was a seriously skewed understanding of who I was as a student, as a person. As a parting gift, he left me with yet another conversation we clearly both remembered.

"It's okay," he consoled me on my last day of elementary school when I was not among the half of my grade to receive a Presidential Academic Fitness Award. "Not everyone is good at school. It's just not for everyone. At least you're good at soccer."

Unfortunately, life in a small town meant that I was not done with Mr. Wallace's opinions of me just yet. My next math teacher had to move me from the lowest level class, where Mr. Wallace had placed me, into the top one. I also met him again on the athletic field, when he was the coach for my failed attempt to play the only soccer available in the school: the boys' team.

Mr. Wallace sought me out one last time, on the lawn of the Community House immediately after I delivered my high school graduating class's valedictory address, exactly thirty years after my mother had done the same. To his credit, he apologized, and I will always remember that as well.

"It seems like you proved me wrong."

I don't remember if I responded or not, but I wish now that I had thanked him, not for the admission, but for his actions. He gave me a reason to work hard, something to fight against, and my first taste of adversity and overcoming an obstacle. Had it not been for my experience with him, I may have crumbled when my first paper in college, one I spent days working on, was returned to me with no grade, only a comment: "Do not give me another paper until you learn to write one." Instead, I signed up for the only writing class offered at the elite liberal arts institution, one for non-native speakers, and considered it to be just another bump along the road.

Part Two

THE BLACKBOARD JUMBLE

(High School Isn't Reality)

Part Three

EDUCATION

Chapter 11
A TILTED PLAYING FIELD

(John, 17 years old)

1964: The Civil Rights Act outlaws discrimination based on race, color, religion, sex or national origin; The Warren Report announces that Lee Harvey Oswald was the lone assassin of President John F. Kennedy; three civil rights workers are murdered in Mississippi; Congress approves the Gulf of Tonkin Resolution, effectively escalating the Vietnam Conflict; Nelson Mandela is imprisoned in South Africa.

On a perfectly sunny, blue sky, green lawn, birds singing, June day, on the cement steps leading up to the red brick Community House, in the center of a perfect New England factory town, those who were about to graduate from the local high school were saluting the flag and listening to an out of tune version of "Pomp and Circumstance."

They sat sweating in caps and gowns, blue for the boys, white for the girls. The band played, and the politician-educators mumbled tips for achieving the American Dream to the blind applause of parents, some of whom had not been allowed to work in this town, some who were underpaid and underappreciated in the shop, some who were not allowed to swim in the town pond, or even pass the doors into this Community House.

Some of the parents had expected this outcome from the time their perfect Unitarians entered kindergarten; others were pleasantly surprised at the outcome; still others were perfectly stupefied and would say a rosary of thanks tonight.

Then, in "apparently fair" alphabetical order, the senior class was called one by one into the presence of education royalty, Principal Waltrip Sidebottom, as the birds chirped and the occasional passing car honked its horn in appreciation or derision. It is so hard to tell the difference.

I don't know if everyone could hear it, or just some, or just me, but as Sidebottom called my name there seemed to be a pronounced emphasis on the first syllable of my last name.

"John Hour-ihan" he said.

I rose from my seat and walked to the front. He looked directly into my eyes and smiled broadly.

He shoved his hand toward me. "Congratulations John," he hissed for the crowd. We both knew full well that the diploma was a blank piece of white paper with my name typed in the center.

I had just listened to a speech by the valedictorian of our class, herself descended from an Italian shop worker, pleading for the town to recognize the right to fairness and equality for everyone, and this fool, the top of the education food chain in our town, was laughing because they had managed to be unfair to me because, as he said himself, I was an Irish punk from Milford.

Determined to keep up the appearance of normalcy for all those watching I shook his hand, smiled, and, as a breeze blew across my face, I said two words. One was a verb, one was a pronoun.

The farce of my "graduation" had started about a week earlier.

I had never had the displeasure of having old and angry Mrs. Crow for a class, but I had been stuck in one of her study halls. My brother

Dennis had had trouble with her, and I figured he was dealing with the same things I was.

It was only a few days before senior release day, and I was finishing up some paperwork for Worcester Junior College. Most people called it Whoopie-J. I had had not so good grades, but decent SATs, and I had managed to get in because the interviewer said he, "had never had an unsolicited teacher go out of her way to write a letter of denigration before, so I wanted to talk to you myself."

My French teacher, Mrs. Mancini, who had determined I was "too stupid to learn a language," had decided it was her job to make sure I didn't get into college.

It seemed that her attempt would work the opposite way.

The only word I saw upside down on his desk was "abomination."

Then it echoed in the assembly room where we were having a study hall, "Hourihan, get up here."

I had become hardened to this ironic manner by which most of the teachers called me to their desks, polite respect being what they taught but not what they practiced.

"Take this to the office." She handed me a folded up piece of math paper.

In the hall I opened it.

It read, "What are we going to do about the Hourihan problem? I would like a decision today."

I turned and walked back to the study hall. If she wanted to hurt my brother, she wasn't going to use me to do it.

I tossed the paper on her desk. "Do I look like a delivery service to you?"

"How dare you, young man? Did you read that?"

"Of course I read it. There isn't a kid in this school who wouldn't have read it, and you know that. You want my brother thrown out of school and you want me to deliver the message, what kind of jerk are you?"

Most of the thirty or so students in the study hall applauded.

She took the note to the office herself in an angry flurry. It seems the school authorities forgot all about Dennis, but within minutes I had been suspended for two weeks.

So close.

Since graduation was in one week, I would have to take my final exams after the two-week banishment.

Hence the blank diploma and the broad smile from the man who had just pontificated about how proud he was of this class. I guess he didn't mean my class.

A few days later I got a call at home. My mother was surprised.

"It's Mr. Drisko, the assistant principal." She shrugged as she handed me the kitchen phone.

"Hello?"

"John?"

"Yes."

"John I just thought it would be fair if I let you know that your exams will not be the same ones your class got."

"OK, I expected that, Mr. D."

"No ... They are ... harder ... if you understand what I'm saying. ... You had better study."

"Yeah Mr. D, so how's that fair?"

"Well ... I just thought you should know."

"Thanks," I said, uncertain if it was the appropriate response.

I studied. I aced the exams in English, biology, and ancient history. Got nothing wrong. Got Bs, begrudgingly.

On the way out of the school for the last time, I stopped into the principal's office to thank Mr. Drisko for the warning. As always, he had done his best to level out a tilted playing field.

They mailed me my diploma a few weeks later, and I was ready to try again.

Chapter 12
USE WELL THY FREEDOM

(Mandy, 18 years old))

1994: Nelson Mandela is elected president of South Africa; television viewers watch for hours as O.J. Simpson in his white Bronco leads police cars on a low-speed chase after he was charged with the murder of his ex-wife and her friend; Olympic figure skater Nancy Kerrigan is attacked with a crowbar; 27 year old Kurt Cobain commits suicide; ER and Friends debut on NBC.

"Wasn't there a building there yesterday?" I asked my new roommate as we passed a part of campus that evoked no sense of familiarity, even though I was sure we had visited it the previous day.

"Maybe. I'm not sure," she answered.

We had woken up for the first time in Willets room 130 at 7:50 in the morning, thanks to her alarm clock, and we filled our coffee mugs from my one-cup machine, before throwing on gym shorts and T-shirts and running out the door in hopes of arriving at our eight o'clock orientation meeting on time. The caffeine had not yet coursed through our veins when we crested the hill and turned around Parrish Hall, but still, I knew something was different. Squinting into the sun, we watched the end of the line of our new classmates file into the LPAC auditorium, and we sped to a sprint, catching the door just before it shut completely, successfully slipping in with the others.

"Wasn't there a building there yesterday?" I repeated toward the end of the line.

"I don't know. I don't think we were on this side of campus yesterday," someone answered, and then noticing our free Earthlust mugs we'd collected at an activity fair the day before, continued. "You have coffee! I wish I'd thought of filling up a mug on the way out of Sharples."

We smiled, knowing that poor soul not only didn't have coffee, but had at least thirty minutes less sleep than we had enjoyed after wasting it at the dining hall. I'd never been one to take a long time in the morning, by teenage girl standards at least, but I'd also never made it to my destination, coffee in hand, within ten minutes of rolling out of bed. It was the first of many positive ways my freshman roommate influenced my life, and I enjoyed my new found freedom. Outside of the occasional wedding and formal event, I have not applied make-up or done more to my hair than brushing it into a ponytail ever since.

We found seats just as Bob Gross, Dean of Students, began to address the 320-member class of 1998 for the first time. "Good morning and welcome to the Swarthmore College Class of 1998," he began. "I'm going to start this morning with a little exercise. I need you to stand up when something I say applies to you." A chorus of groans ensued, no one wanted to stand up when the night had ended so recently. Our first night on campus had extended well into the morning. It was one of awkward encounters with future friends, of computer challenges - it turns out we had a new technology called email right in our dorm rooms, but it didn't work until we plugged a telephone cord into BOTH the computer and the wall, and of spontaneous discussions of more depth than I had ever experienced.

Bob persisted. "Stand up if you scored a perfect 1600 on your SATs." I looked around the air-conditioned auditorium, and an alarming number of my classmates rose. Bob paused, and my self-consciousness escalated. "Stand up if you were class valedictorian." Phew! I shot up with pride and relief to be in the company of those standing already. He continued, "Stand up if you were president of your class. Stand up if you were the captain of a sports team. Stand up if you scored a five on at least one AP test. Stand up if you were first chair in the band. Stand up if you started a club in your high school." He continued with statement of similar accolades, clearly calculated to insure everyone's inclusion. I tried not to be caught looking as I stole quick glances left and to my right. "Look around you," Bob continued. "That's right. Everyone is standing," he paused for a minute, allowing nervous laughter to fill the air, as we soaked in the caliber of our new class and our rightful spots in it. "Now sit down." I was unclear about whether the point of the activity was to build us up or knock us down. More likely, it was both.

"You all had incredible high school careers or you wouldn't be here," he continued. "But high school is over, and you are about to embark upon a new endeavor. It won't always be easy, but I don't want you ever to forget how special you all are. So repeat after me: 'No matter what you say or do to me, I am still a worthwhile person.'"

A couple people spoke, but more giggled, awkwardly, so he repeated his request.

"I know it's early, but join me here. 'No matter what you say or do to me, I am still a worthwhile person.'"

Through our chuckles, we parroted his words.

"There will be days when you go into Sharples by yourself. You get your tray and collect your food, and then you will walk into the big room and look around it. You will see no one you know, no familiar and friendly face to join for your meal. You will try the middle room, and maybe even the small room, and then you will give up and sit by yourself, staring out the window toward Mertz Lawn. And when that happens, I want you to hear my words. Repeat after me: 'No matter what you say or do to me, I am still a worthwhile person.'"

We dutifully repeated.

This continued while he described scenarios of social rejection, something we already knew, and of academic failure, which we did not yet understand. Each time, he made us repeat his phrase:

"No matter what you say or do to me, I am still a worthwhile person."

It became a sort of tongue-in-cheek mantra as college progressed, one which was repeated four years later in the build up to graduation, and one we all remembered, in our own ways. For me, I credit it, along with the words carved into the east wing of Parrish Hall, "Use well thy freedom," as the two best pieces of advice I received in the next four years, during which I was privileged enough to live, study and play at the pinnacle of American liberal arts education.

And yes, there had been a building there the previous day; it had been taken down with a wrecking ball overnight, and after a year or so, the orange construction fencing would be replaced with Kohlberg Hall, its "runway" lit path and infamous art glass windows.

Chapter 13
A BRIDGE TOO FAR

(John, 18 years old))

1965: First U.S. combat troops arrive in Vietnam; an avalanche destroys a mining village and shuts Hyder, Alaska off from the rest of the state.

I wore my gray three-button, winter, Salvation Army Thrift Shop sport coat to the first day at Woopie J and sat in the front row of every class. I was the only one in English class to catch the use of the word "humorous" as meaning watering in the eyes of the turtle in Grapes of Wrath that told he was walking full-force west into the setting sun not listening to jokes, and History of Western Civilization was pretty much the same as it had been in history class in the fifth and seventh grades at St. Mary's. I listened, I took notes, and I studied. I ended the year with a 3.6 GPA, a new girlfriend, a new home (I was now living with my sister Pat and her new and soon-to-be-ex husband so I could study.) I spent weekends at my parents' house, driving my sister's red VW Beetle and drinking with Joe Bilagio and some other old high school friends.

My world had changed so much that I asked for and got a date with the valedictorian of our high school class. I think, for her part, it was because we were both living out of town and no one would know. It was so passionate that I had had two teeth pulled that day and she never knew. We went to an Elvis Presley movie, and I got a nice handshake goodnight.

This spawned a new rule: know which people want to be with you. And which ones just want you to pay the way.

At my parents' home, Thursdays had changed to every day.

My father's drinking had been the major cause of his heart attack my senior year of high school, and now, since his heart attack had ended his working career, he had a lot more time to drink.

One Friday, in Hopedale during dinner, Scrapper Jack rolled out of a cab in front of our middle class home in the suburbs. Inside the house, were ice-like hard-wood floors, a shining chandelier, a player piano, a heating system that blew warm air out like a steady wind, and toilets that flushed. Outside it had peeling gray paint and a fright-wig lawn. It was 6 p.m. the sun was bright, and he was beyond drunk. I poked at my Brussels sprouts with a fork while I watched him stumble from the car to the driveway to the lawn, lawn to the drive, back and forth up the driveway. Even though I knew what was coming, it was pretty comical.

We had been able to move to Hopedale, the town where my mother's family had lived when she was a girl, mainly because three of my sisters, with the exception of the oldest, were forced to drop out of high school and go to work at the shoe shop. With their paychecks added to my mother's and what my father brought home sometimes from card games, there was enough money for the move up. Somehow in the vertical jump we had lost a lot of what had been our way of life. There were sacrifices we had made to acquire stuff we probably didn't need. My sisters had been yanked from high school to go to the shop, my mother had returned to work, and my father was devastated that he was not supporting his family at all because he was sick and weak for the first time in his life. In retaliation my sisters jumped ship, I had moved out, Dennis was a recluse, and family dinner was a thing of the past. We had lost St. Mary's and we had lost Purchase Street.

I looked across the kitchen table and said to my mother, "Dad's home."

I watched her deflate from the contentment of having her son home to the uncertainty and anxiety of having her husband home.

As he stumbled in the front door, his first attack was directed at my sister Nancy who was visiting. She was coming down the stairs from the bathroom and stood on the third step face to face with three sheets to the wind.

"You fucking girls all turned out to be sluts," he slurred. The word sluts sounded more like Schlitz, but we all knew what he meant. "You know you were supposed to get married *before* you got pregnant. And then half of you had to marry wops. Couldn't keep your knees together?"

It was an unfair and unwarranted attack. Pretty much, three of my sisters had one-by-one gotten married in self defense. And Nancy wasn't pregnant when she got married. The oldest used college. It was difficult to reconcile our love for a wonderful man, who taught us all to have a social conscience, with the fear of his Bizarro self when he drank.

I stood up from the table. "That's enough!" I shouted.

He turned to me, surprised that I had said anything. Since I was six years old and stood between him and my mother while he was screaming and subconsciously wielding a butter knife, I hadn't said anything during his tirades. At that time I just took the knife away, put it in the silverware drawer and went and sat down on the kitchen floor

Usually we all just listened until he was done and then left the room. He opened his mouth, but I talked first. "Don't bring that barroom bullshit into this house. Leave it where you were this afternoon. We've had enough of your crap … since we were born … No more!"

With hands like steel vice grips he grabbed me around the throat and forced me against the wall.

"You think you can take me? You don't have a fucking chance."

He never swore when he was sober.

My mother stepped in and grabbed his right arm.

"Jack," she shouted. "Get ahold of yourself. He's right, this isn't a barroom. And he's your son, and he will fight. You just stop."

He let go and looked at me with the angry eyes of an Irishman who had been challenged by someone who had been a disappointment to him his whole life. Not good enough in basketball, not tough enough, didn't have enough women, and had even given up his best sport, baseball. Nothing his oldest son had done so far had impressed him enough.

I looked back and before he could speak I said, "Fists aren't the only thing that works. I'm telling you, leave my sisters alone."

Looking at his eyes I saw the other side of Scrapper Jack. His eyes watered, and I knew he was judging himself more harshly than I ever could. I pushed him back a step and walked past him.

Nancy was sitting on the stairs. It was the first time I had had the honor of defending a person who had defended me all my life.

"Go home Nancy," I said, "You don't have to take this shit anymore."

Neither did I.

I left the house and walked the four miles to town. I met up with Larry, a friend who wanted to be a cop. We drove to Woonsocket where we met with Larry's friend "Reb" at a hamburger stand. "Reb" was in his late 20s, originally from Mississippi and had moved up to Rhode Island a few months earlier to work on the pipeline that was going through. Larry told me Reb had been seeing someone in our area. "He's a good guy," Larry told me. "This woman he's seeing has a kid and he doesn't even care."

Reb bought us a case of beer, and we went on our way.

The next day, severely hung over, I went to the Air Force recruiter in the Milford Town Hall. He was at lunch so I joined the Army – something my father had never been allowed to do, flat feet, too many kids.

I figured I'd put in thirty years and get out at forty-nine with a good pension and half my life ahead of me. It was a way up the ladder.

Within a handful of weeks I was bused from the Boston Army Base to Fort Dix, New Jersey. I was Private E1 Hourihan. I don't remember ever saying a meaningful sentence to my father again.

On our nearly impossible quest to move out of poverty we had lost our way. We had lost our family.

Chapter 14
YOU MIGHT NOT GET
THERE FROM HERE

(Mandy, 19 years old)

1995: Timothy McVeigh is arrested for bombing the Oklahoma City Federal Building; Israeli Prime Minister Yitzhak Rabin is killed by extremists at a peace rally; millions watch as a not guilty verdict is delivered to OJ Simpson; Grateful Dead front man Jerry Garcia dies.

I spent spring break during my freshman year in Antigua, with my roommate and our friend, experiencing the ups and downs of a social class to which I would never belong. Her parents were amazing, so warm, kind and generous, and we enjoyed a week in our own room at their fancy resort overlooking the endless blue sea. Morning room service offered fresh tropical fruit and the best croissants I have ever tasted. Dinner lasted for five full courses every night, and they patiently taught me rules of etiquette that I never thought I'd need to know. We took sailing lessons with a hot young instructor, and when they learned of my love for the Kennedys, arrangements were made to meet Ted and Vicky for dinner. Although the plans fell through, I thoroughly appreciated their thoughtfulness and efforts. Other guests were less accepting, however. Although I attended a fancy liberal arts college, I still received scornful looks when admitting that I attended an unknown, public high school.

We just laughed.

Despite an awful sunburn that left me permanently scarred from my first and last attempt at wearing a bikini, I returned from spring break confident and rejuvenated, ready to attack the end of my freshman year, ready for something new. I had considered playing basketball that winter, but the length of the season intimidated me, and the softball coach had asked me to join her team because they only had ten players. After passing on that opportunity in favor of my Antigua vacation, I thought I had missed out once and for all on team sports that year, and they had been a part of my life since I was six years old. Monday afternoon as I sat in the lounge of our dorm, my friend Ashley came through with cleats in her hand. I had never heard Ashley talking about field sports before, so I was surprised, and I asked her where she was going. She explained that she was going to play Ultimate Frisbee, although no, she hadn't really worn cleats in years, if ever. She had only played a few times, and she assured me that I'd be welcome. I was looking for an activity, and a way to procrastinate from the endless piles of books I had to read, so I grabbed my cleats and headed to Mertz Lawn for the first time.

I laced up my cleats that afternoon completely unaware of how much both that split-second decision to try Ultimate and my emerging friendship with Ashley would shape my life.

When I arrived, I had no idea how to throw a Frisbee. None. I had never even tossed one around on the beach. One captain taught me how to hold it to throw a forehand and a backhand and patiently chased after each errant throw with a seemingly omnipresent smile on her face. I followed along in a few drills, resigned to be the worst one there. In the final drill of the day, we were instructed to cut from the front of a line for the first catch, and then to time a cut off the back of the line to be ready to receive it when the first person had made the catch. I couldn't throw or catch, but years of soccer, field hockey and basketball had more than prepared me for a simple cut. The second captain, who had arrived late that day, was leading this drill. Her growing frustration with the group's inability to conduct the drill properly had become evident, and she jumped to the front of the first line just as I took my proper turn in the back of the line. I started my cut as the first throw was in the air, planted, turned, and arrived in perfect time for the disc to bounce awkwardly off my hands and land in the mud.

"Stop, stop, stop!"

I froze with fear.

"That's it! That's right! That's what I've been trying to tell you! You, what's your name?"

"Mandy."

"Mandy, go back to the end of the stack. Can you do that again?"

"Sure," I really wasn't sure what was so good about what I had done. I made a simple cut and dropped a Frisbee. The captain returned to the front to demonstrate her "handler" cut, and I repeated my actions several times, never once catching the Frisbee. Still, I seemed to have done something right.

I learned that afternoon that the team had only existed for about a year, and they were all still learning. The captains were only sophomores, and they had played with the men's team as freshmen before starting the team with several friends. They invited me to my first tournament that weekend, twenty minutes down the road at Haverford. I modestly reminded them that I couldn't throw or catch, but they were undeterred, and with that, I found myself stepping onto a fifteen passenger van with seventeen other Swatties at seven o'clock Saturday morning, only one week after I had been swimming in the Caribbean.

I also found myself stepping off that van in the breakdown lane of the Interstate about fifteen minutes later, when black smoke enveloped us.

We took pictures, we tried to throw a Frisbee on the side of the Blue Route, which was utterly unsuccessful because I was not the only one who couldn't throw or catch, and eventually, we composed lyrics to the tune of some "Plastic Jesus on the Dashboard" song someone knew:

> "First the boys' team flew right by us,
> Then the track team, they denied us,
> Seven cop cars came to stare and gawk ..."

There was more, but I'm not sure why I remember even that much. My father says that sometimes time bends a little, and you remember something that should be inconsequential at the time because it ends up having significance later. Perhaps that's the case.

We arrived very late to Haverford, even by "Ultimate time," but that day I played my first official Ultimate Frisbee tournament, alongside a friend with whom I would eventually explore our nation, at the home of my future husband whom I had not yet met.

Over the next three and a half years I played Ultimate Frisbee more days than not. I practiced Monday-Thursday on Mertz Lawn and played co-ed pick-up every Friday. I played a tournament every weekend in the spring and fall, leagues in the summer, and indoors in the winter, even at midnight on Valentine's Day immediately after breaking up with a boyfriend. I never learned to throw very well, but I did learn that my speed and ability to read the disc allowed me to catch just about anything and defend just about anyone. I made lasting friendships and served as college captain for two years. I planned practices, tournaments, and road trips. I rented vans and told my teammates to arrive at 6:30 when we didn't need to leave until 7:00 so we wouldn't be late. I applied for my first credit card to purchase fundraising merchandise, studied the game and the Ultimate Players' Association standings, called subs and set strategies, booked hotel rooms and campsites, secured funding from the college and gym credit for the players, turned in meal numbers and collected turkey sandwiches, chips, apples and juice boxes from

Sharples, drank way too much beer out of Frisbees (it holds six cans, if you're careful enough), learned how to tape ankles and take Advil for knees, maintained my fitness to play almost every point of seven competitive games in two days, and had the most unadulterated fun of my life.

In the Swarthmore "Warmothers" Ultimate Frisbee team, I found my home. For the first time in my life, I felt free to be completely myself, and not only did I never feel judged for it, but the more I was true to myself, the more my friendships with my teammates grew. It gave me confidence both on and off the field, and that newfound confidence spread throughout my life. I started taking honors seminars, participating in class discussions, and taking on leadership roles around campus. I had my first real boyfriend, and then I broke up with him because I wanted more time to play Frisbee. Then I started dating within the team, but even that took too much time from my true passion. I continued to play Ultimate after I graduated, and the sport has brought me all over North America, from Florida to Montreal, from Wildwood on the Jersey Shore to O'ahu's Waiminalo Beach, from Tucson to Boulder and to Poultry Days. Perhaps most notably, it brought me to Mardi Gras. Twice. Where I nearly got arrested once, but didn't because my father had taught me, "When the cops come, run like hell." It worked.

I poured all of myself into the team and so did many of my teammates. There is nothing quite like being all-in to something you love, together. For my efforts, I earned two awards that remain among my most cherished: a beer mug, engraved "Mandy: The Ultimate Warmother," given by my team upon my graduation, and my Co-ed Senior vs. Underclassmen Game MVP award, given for a lay-out grab. It is a crumpled piece of corrugated cardboard, with the text of the cheer from the game scribbled in Sharpee on one side and "MVP: Mandy" written in pencil on the back.

Chapter 15
PLAYING THE CARDS

(John, 19-20 years old))

1966: The Supreme Court decides Miranda vs. Arizona, protecting the rights of the accused; DNA code first deciphered; "The Pill" determined to be safe for humans.

Basic training at nineteen was as easy as Wally's girlfriend.

Instead of the pretense I lived with in Hopedale, that everyone was being treated fairly when, in fact, some were being singled out for different treatment, the reality at Fort Dix was that everyone was very obviously being treated like shit, no exceptions, and that was something I could deal with. I saw it as the game it was and waltzed through. Like Woody said, "Deal me your hardest hand and I'll win this God damn game."

Then, the night before we would all head home on leave, Victor Company trainees sat cross-legged on the perfectly waxed and buffed floor of the day room somewhere in the middle of Fort Dix. Sgt. Malone, the giant black man, and Sgt. Callahan, a short, fireplug, blond crew cut Irishman, stood in front of us.

Malone, our head drill sergeant, spoke.

"Now that yous have put in your eight weeks' time, yous mens is on a even par with the Army mule," he said.

This was where we would each find out where we would be going for advanced training, but first he read off a list of names who had received accelerated promotions. I stood up with the rest of the ten percent of the company who for one reason or another had just become E2 privates a step above the damn mule. Everyone would catch up as soon as they got to their next duty station, but we "elite" would get an extra month's raise in pay.

My test grades had put me in the Army Security Agency, a military arm of NSA. When Malone got to reading my orders, he lapsed out of his practiced air of feigned stupidity into just being himself.

"Well Private Hourihan, we have some good news, some better news, and some not so good news." He smiled at me. It was his recommendation that had afforded me the promotion for being the top marksman in our company. "Your tests put you in the top three percent of the Army … Further testing put you in the Defense Language Institute in California." He lowered the papers he was reading from, "That's the top one percent, trainee … I'm impressed, and here is the not so good part. You'll be studying Vietnamese."

His eyebrows raised.

I had no idea why this was such a bad thing and asked, "What the hell is Viennese? I didn't ask for that. I asked for French."

A murmur turned quickly into laughter by all those other recruits who were not in the top one percent or even the top three percent. All those "dummies" knew where Vietnam was, unlike those of us who had been educated in an inadequate, pompous for no apparent reason education system taught by teachers, many of whom hid the world from us while they plied their own prejudices and biases and got us ready for work in the foundry of The Diamond D, Draper Corporation. At least that's what I blamed it on.

It dawned on me in a particularly frigid mid-December, in the day room of Victor Company, Fort Dix, that I had just signed up for four years in the U.S. Army in 1965, and I didn't even know that we were at war. Guess I wasn't paying attention.

Our second drill instructor, Sgt Callahan, stepped up and incredulously spouted, "You be in this man's army, headed for Vietnam, and you don't know where it is? Tell me boy that you know we are at war. Tell me you isn't that fucking stupid. Please, tell me you knew."

I hadn't, "I do now, Sarge."

Every trainee laughed. Both DIs laughed. I laughed. It wasn't funny.

And my first rule in the Army was born. Have a sense of humor, and play the cards you're dealt.

I drank away a month of leave in the town where I had dodged or been hidden from the knowledge that my country was at war in Vietnam, and I headed for Monterey, Calif. to learn the language of our enemy because I was so smart.

After six weeks or so of trying my best to flunk out of school, myself and a handful of others with similar ideas were called in and the Major explained, "We can't flunk you out. It would be better for you if you learned the language."

I set up chairs for the Monterey Jazz Festival - made ten bucks, got recruited by a Baha'i girl until she realized I was only in it for her. I met a Playboy bunny who tried to teach me to surf and then took me to a beach party where the guitar-playing singer among the fifteen or so partiers was Joan Baez. I traveled California on the back of a motorcycle, Yosemite to Salinas to Big Sur. Saw Elizabeth Taylor at a restaurant on Cannery Row. I sang at the Gas Light Lounge of a Ramada Inn. They paid me in beer until it got too costly and they decided to pay me $50 a performance to save money. I got promoted again, spent whole days sunning on Carmel Beach, and tried to drink the EM Club dry. Then on leave at home, on a particularly warm and decidedly marijuana-mind-altered afternoon with Mike and Peter, my best friends in Hopedale, we pulled the car into a restaurant parking lot, slid down the steep grass-and-dirt hill to the water and went swimming in a lake beside the highway. While Mike and Peter swam, my attention was taken by two girls on the bank. I made my way to shore, sat on a shore rock and talked with them for a few minutes. I found out that the blond was named "Spooky" and the pretty dark-haired one with the teal blue eyes lived in the red house on the hill across the highway, when my friends came and grabbed me and told me it was time to go. "She's like 12 years old," Pete warned. That I hadn't noticed, so we left, and I went back to California.

In the meantime in California, I learned the damn language, packed my duffel bag and went to their war – Specialist Fourth Class Hourihan. Vietnamese linguist, just playing the cards I was dealt.

Chapter 16
DEATH CHANGES EVERYTHING

(Mandy, 19-20 years old))

1996: U.S. and Russian troops enter Bosnia in a joint operation; the first version of the Java programming language is released; Marge Schott gives up day-to-day operations of her major league baseball team because of her comments about Hitler, working women, and Asians.

By junior year I had hit my stride at Swarthmore. I had arguably the best dorm room on campus, a three-room quad with a bay window overlooking Wharton courtyard, and I shared it with three of my best friends. We bunked the beds, squeezed as much furniture as we could into the tiny side rooms, and found a futon for the enormous middle room so we could enjoy our own private lounge. I had my first real boyfriend that fall, my friend Gabi and I were the newly elected captains of the Ultimate team, and I even tackled my first honors seminar. I had achieved what I saw as the benchmark set for me on day one: I walked confidently into Sharples at any hour of the day, always knowing I'd find a room full of friendly faces with whom to sit. On the rare occasion on which I didn't, I sat by myself, gazing over Mertz Lawn, content with my solitude and my view. My life matched the idyllic setting in which it was transpiring, and I relished every minute of the world it allowed me to create.

Thanksgiving approached. Thanksgiving has always been my favorite holiday. Growing up I enjoyed it for the extended family celebration, for the enormity of the meal, for its alignment with my birthday, which added gifts to the equation, for the extra time with my mother the day before when she would take the day off to bake, and the day after when we would brave Black Friday sales long before the days of midnight madness. As an adult I have shared the holiday as a potluck with friends, and I have extended it into a three-day extravaganza with my step-brother's family. In college, I typically tried to plan my fall course schedule so I could steal a weeklong vacation for the holiday, and junior year had been no different.

However, as the days passed, my trepidation rose. During the previous summer, my mother had asked my father for a divorce, and within days of my return to campus, he had moved out. In the aftermath, my brother had changed his college plans completely, choosing to begin his career near home and with friends at UMass, Dartmouth, instead of joining me in my adopted home state as a Penn State freshman. Not only would this Thanksgiving be completely different, it would establish a new family order, and serve as the beginning of the rest of my life. I had no interest in allowing anyone else to define that life for me, nor was I yet sure how I wanted it to look. The longer I stayed in my Swarthmore life, the longer I could postpone the inevitable.

One week before I'd be driving back to Hopedale, I no longer wanted to leave campus at all. In a fit of a panic and indecision, at midnight on a Friday night I knocked on the door of the friend whose future as a counselor was already evident. I had seen less of her junior year, as she spent more time with her boyfriend, who was one of my very first college friends. Always up for shooting a basketball or playing intramural soccer, he was as enthralled with club volleyball as I was with club Ultimate. I had tried emailing and calling her, but she hadn't replied within the hour or two I allowed, and when she answered the door, her face revealed why. I started to apologize for harassing her when she clearly had something upsetting her, but she had expected me, and she found words first, telling me of her boyfriend's recent diagnosis of multiple sclerosis, a disease that typically attacks middle-aged women, not teenage boys.

After talking to her, I stopped by his room. He needed a ride north for the holiday. We decided to drive up Saturday morning, and back the following Saturday. His illness knocked my struggles into focus, and without having made that choice for its own sake, I left for Thanksgiving after all. I did not stay at my old house, opting instead for the spare room of a gracious older friend with whom I had worked over the summer, and arrived at my childhood home only long enough for the meal itself. I skipped the baking, skipped my birthday, and avoided the shopping trip by fabricating a story requiring my return to campus on Friday. My alibi crumbled with my friend's call to my mother's house to double check logistics for Saturday's drive back to campus, and my mother, in turn, called me in tears of disbelief, seeking an explanation I felt she shouldn't need and an apology she never received.

During the six hour drive back, we shared previously undisclosed details about the changes the past few months had unexpectedly delivered us each and about our fears for their impact on our lives. While I was able to navigate the bumps along the way and settle into a new normal, his case turned out to be worse than he allowed himself to imagine or admit at the time, and he succumbed to the disease about ten years after we graduated. He had moved to Arizona with his family by then and had lost touch with most college friends. I should have known something was wrong when he stopped responding to our roughly every-other-month email exchange that we had maintained through the years, but instead I learned of his passing through the alumni notes, almost nine months later.

Chapter 17
WELCOME TO THE
CHILDREN'S WAR

(John, 20 years old))

1967: Woody Guthrie dies; NSA builds a listening post on Diego Garcia in an attempt to enhance the 'worldwide Advanced Tactical Ocean Surveillance System' along with many other important facilities around the globe; because of better intelligence the NSA was able to provide warning of a huge North Vietnamese buildup before the Tet offensive.

The Northwest Orient civilian pilot had a joke to welcome us to Vietnam.

"This is the captain. We are making our approach to Tan Son Nhut Airbase, currently the busiest airport in the civilized world. The temperature is, let's see, 104 Fahrenheit. It is dry, windy and sunny, and there is moderate to heavy ground fire. Welcome to the Paris of the Orient boys."

If I had known what the next three years held I would have gone up to the cockpit and beat him senseless.

We had landed in Honolulu, Hawai'i on the way, God's country, but we weren't allowed to get off the plane. Then, a long airborne sleep later, it was February 1967, I was twenty years old, two years younger than the twenty-two year old average age of our combat vets, including all the officers and veteran NCOs, and I had arrived at the war. In WWII the average age of a soldier was twenty-six.

The heat from the tarmac hit us fiercely in the face as we walked in small groups toward the huddle of buildings in front of us.

The crush of sweating soldiers in the terminal was an entire crowd of uniformed kids, many of them younger than I was, looking lost and frightened and hoping for someone to tell them what they were supposed to do next. We had seen it all on TV, but this was the real place. The young soldiers mingled with civilian Vietnamese selling, begging or travelling, with combat vets on their way home, and with Korean and Australian soldiers heavily armed and looking dangerous. I don't know why, but somehow I wasn't scared, not even a little.

I followed a guy with a sign "509th Radio Research Group" to an Army Jeep parked outside. When he dropped me off about fifteen minutes later at Davis Station he pointed at a small building. "That's HQ. Go sign in." That night I slept on a cot, in a tent, in the middle of a parking lot outside HQ, with a dozen or so other new guys, and in the morning, covered with so many mosquito bites it looked like a rash, I was flown to the 313th RR Battalion up country on the coast in Nha Trang.

It didn't take long for the novelty to wear off. After only three weeks of doing mindless busy-work while waiting for Personnel to get around to cutting orders for our group of 330th Radio Research Company linguists and ditty-boppers, those who intercepted Morse Code, to go further up country to Pleiku, the futility of it all just got to me one morning.

I sat on a warm sandbag wall that wrapped protectively around a tent and lit a cigarette. I was in a hurry to get to the war. I had heard promotions came more easily there, and I was eager to climb up the military ladder. How hard could it be, I thought. And then we got stuck doing monkey work in a rear area.

"Hourihan, get to work. You think you're special?" I would hear that a lot now that I was in the ASA. It was kind of a kick that most Army personnel thought those of us in our outfit had reason to think we were special.

"We're filling plastic bags with sand, sergeant. How special can that be?"

"Sandbags will save your life in a mortar attack," he offered.

"Sure, but we are getting the sand for these bags out of other sandbags. This isn't safety, this is bull shit."

"For two cents I'd kick your ass, troop."

I just couldn't stop myself. I fished through my fatigue pants pocket, pulled out a five-cent Military Payment Certificate. I crumpled it, tossed it to the stunned non-com and said, "Here's a nickel, let's see what you got."

After review by the Commanding Officer, our orders were cut the next day, and I got a slap on the back from the CO and the thanks of my new buddies.

My new home was a General Purpose Medium tent, one of dozens plunked in lines in the powdered red clay of the central highlands. We were a few miles from the tri-border area where the countries of Vietnam, Laos and Cambodia meet, the place where the Ho Chi Minh trail, named after the North Vietnamese leader, entered Vietnam, carrying with it the supplies for all the North Vietnamese troops and Viet Cong militia in the south.

Pleiku was a hot spot in the war, a good place where you could melt away any values or principles you still had. And, for a while I did.

My workstation at the 330th was where I was headed after dropping off my duffel, an M14 - 7.62 mm, gas operated, fully automatic, hand cannon, a bayonet and six magazines of ammo at my cot inside Tent 8. I counted seven other cots inside, then followed my trick chief back down the powder-dirt road through the company area toward the Operations Compound where I would be working.

In the last war, Specialist 5 Donald Isa would have been in the 442, a segregated outfit that was made up of Japanese Hawaiians. In this war he was where he should be, the supervisor of a bunch of Army Security Agency electronic spies.

The operations area was as long and wide as half a football field of red talcum dirt surrounded by concertina wire piled fifteen feet high. The only opening was at the Military Police guard shack where we had to flash our Worldwide Security Badge for entrance. The shack had an M-60 machine gun mounted on top, pointed suspiciously at the operations compound itself. Inside the circle of barbed wire and, later I would find out, several claymore mines, were three Quonset huts. "Home, sweet home," I thought, remembering my home growing up in the barrio of South Phoenix.

This was an Army Security Agency post, disguised as a Radio Research Company. Since Vietnam wasn't yet a declared war, the Geneva Convention rules said the ASA wasn't even supposed to be here. Our work was so secret we weren't allowed to talk about it to anyone outside the operations compound, even to the people who worked right next to us.

"We work in the trucks." Isa pointed to the left where twelve large trucks called deuce-and-a-halfs because they could carry two and a half tons of payload, were backed up to a raised wooden ramp. The camper-type vans in the back of each truck contained work stations where eighteen year olds ran that part of the war that was being fought in the Pleiku area.

We were to be the eyes and ears of all the GIs who ate red clay for breakfast and slept to the murmur of a Spooky gunship's miniguns as they rained down fire on the positions we singled out the day before, like a dragon clearing its throat.

As we reached the last truck on the right, my duty station, Isa and I stood in the door and looked inside. There were two rows of three gray R390 radios each, the size of those new portable TVs, lined up back to back. They were each connected to a reel-to-reel tape recorder. A chair faced each, and there was a typewriter on a metal table in front of each chair.

As I entered I noticed that all five of the men working the van were standing up and surrounding one who was sitting and had a headset on, and a captain was looking over their shoulders.

I knew the guy with the headset. His name was John Caron. He had been in my DLIWC class. To be exact he was near the bottom of our class.

"Well Caron, is it North or South Vietnamese?" the captain asked.

Caron, a recent high school graduate, had only gotten here about three weeks before I did. He passed up his leave and came right over. He looked at me, and I knew immediately he had no idea which accent he was hearing.

"North," he finally said, pulled off the headset and pushed by everyone to say hello to me. The captain swept by us and out the door. The rest went back to work. I was shown the position where I would be intercepting enemy voice transmissions, taping them and transcribing them for the analysts to decode.

"You don't start for a few days," Isa said and walked me back to the Enlisted Men's Club.

After a handful of sweat-drenched days sleeping in a sleeping bag, on a cot, in a tent, with about a thousand mosquitoes, and long nights at the EM Club drinking myself nauseous, I went to work and found out that Caron had guessed wrong, and the artillery on the next hill had blown away a couple platoons of ARVN soldiers by mistake on the say-so of an eighteen year old kid who was one of the guys who had tried to flunk out of language school. This was my introduction to the war. The difference, they said, between the Army and the Boy Scouts was that the Boy Scouts had adult leadership.

It was as if we were all children trying to play parts in a war movie that was written for a whole different era, a different planet. It sure didn't remind me of Marlon Brando, John Wayne or Audie Murphy. It was something entirely different, so, for now, I kept my head down, found out how to get into off-limits Pleiku, became very familiar with the women of the city and the ones who worked at our club. It became obvious that, since I was in Vietnam instead of St. Mary's, I was going to see sex not as a sin but as a gift. I decided to sit out the war. I didn't know the Army wasn't going to let me.

Chapter 18
JUST ALONG FOR THE RIDE

(Mandy, 20 years old)

1997: Hopedale, Massachusetts: In 1842 Adin Ballou founded The Hopedale Community in an effort to use Practical Christianity to achieve a morally superior society with deeply held idealistic beliefs of non-violence, anti-slavery, and women's rights, and with a strong value placed on the role of formal and informal means of education. The Hopedale Community ran until 1856, when its joint-stock was taken over by the Drapers, who developed their company into the second largest textile loom manufacturer by the turn of the century and reshaped the town into a model company town, complete with factory housing and corporately held lands and controlled elections. The southward migration of industry left the factory building vacant by the 1980s, where it still remains as a vacant blight in the center of town.

As junior year drew to a close, I found myself without a major. I had spent the last three years taking classes that interested me. Along the way, my eclectic transcript included classes in engineering, physics, and calculus, titles like "Love and Religion," "Japanese Civilization and Culture," "Murder in a Mill Town," and "The Socio-Economic Roots of Linguistic Biases in Education" (or something like that). What I hadn't done was fulfill the breadth requirements for any major. In order to be able to fill my senior year schedule the same way I had so far, I devised a special major, which I named "History and Education," and my friends lovingly called "Classes I've Already Taken." That left me with only one requirement for senior year: a thesis tying together the pieces of my newly created major. One afternoon I wandered into the Peace Collection in the Swarthmore Library, and discovered a complete set of all twenty years of *The Practical Christian*, Adin Ballou's newspaper from the utopian community that he founded as the initial settlement in Hopedale. After some quick research, I learned that it was the only complete set outside of my hometown, marking the first of many times my seemingly unrelated worlds have aligned. I applied for and received a summer grant from Swarthmore to study the role of formal and informal education through the history of Hopedale, including its inception in the utopian community, its function for the company town, and its redefinition in a post-industrial suburb. The $3,000 grant would cover all the money I needed to earn over the summer to pay for my share of the fall's tuition, as long as I could live for free, so when junior year ended, I returned to my childhood house in Hopedale one last time.

I spent the summer in the safe at Hopedale's Bancroft library whenever it was open and playing Ultimate Frisbee whenever it wasn't. I played an hour north in Chelmsford on Mondays and Wednesdays, an hour east in Somerville on Thursdays, and escaped to tournaments or friends' houses any weekend I could. My mother had put the house on the market, and asked my brother and me to make it available for showings when she was at work during the day. Mike, who had just completed his freshman year of college, was unwilling to open his bedroom door before noon, so on the days with showings, I cleaned the living room and kitchen, ran the dishwasher, and made sure his door was closed before leaving for the library. It was my way of earning my keep.

One week in July, Ashley was visiting from Maine, and my mother was on a business trip in Pennsylvania. Ashley and I had returned from an Ultimate game in Chelmsford and spent the rest of the evening watching TV with Mike. Around midnight, we decided to go upstairs to sleep. She was a few steps in front of me, but we hadn't bothered to turn the hall light on before ascending the carpeted steps of our colonial. She made it to the top, and switched on the light when she thought she had seen something move. We both stopped in our tracks; the steps were lined with bees, apparently sleeping, motionless. There must have been thousands of them. Starting about five steps from the top, they lined every inch of every stair as well as the walls, doors, and floor on the upstairs landing.

Frozen, our eyes grew wide. We were both barefoot, wearing tank tops and gym shorts. It was unclear how either of us had gotten to where we were without stepping on any bees, but there was no visible escape, either up or down.

"MIKE!!!" We yelled. He was still watching TV in the living room, and unlike us, he was wearing baggy jeans and sneakers.

"What?"

"Um ... help?!"

Eyes glued to his show, we were going to have to come up with more context than that. I leaned around the bottom of the half wall, over the banister, and into the living room so I could see him, hoping my face would convey my urgency.

"Come over here!"

Maybe that wasn't the best request.

He rose slowly, taking time to turn off the television, and started toward me.

"What is it?"

"Um ... bees."

"You want me to kill a bee for you?"

"Not exactly."

When Mike got close enough to the railing and finally saw the bees, he walked silently, stoically, right past the stairs. Ashley and I called to him again, but he continued his slow, deliberate pace, in the direction of the garage, and without a word, he disappeared.

A few minutes later he returned with a bottle of carpet cleaner.

"Don't worry, ladies, I'm going to bust you out of here," he declared calmly, as he started spraying carpet cleaner at every surface he could find.

"Michael, what are you doing?!"

"I told you, I'm gonna bust you out of here," he continued to spray every square inch of the stairs, walls, floors, and doors.

Barefoot, Ashley and I hadn't yet moved. I had been hoping for shoes, not carpet cleaner, but I guess if I wanted shoes, I should have asked for them.

As he continued to spray, we began to cough. It didn't smell like carpet cleaner.

"Mike, what are you spraying?" Ashley asked.

"I dunno."

"What do you mean you don't know? What does it say on the bottle?"

"Oh. I dumped that out. I filled it with some bug killing thing I found in the garage. It had a picture of roses on it."

The smell overtook us, and our coughing intensified. Ashley realized that if she could open the door to the bathroom, which was only about one jump away, it may be clear of bees. She did, and we hopped into the bathroom, and from there we passed through the door into what used to be my parents' bedroom. She and I locked ourselves in there, while Mike continued his lethal assault on the bees, which were starting to awaken only long enough to die.

Next to the bed, we found a telephone. It was after midnight, but it was becoming clear that between the bees and whatever chemical was filling our lungs, we couldn't sleep in the house, and neither could Jody, our oversized, poorly-mannered lab-Samoyed mix, who was mysteriously still asleep on the living room couch. Our car was in the driveway, but using it never occurred to us. By the time Mike slipped into the room, shutting the door behind him, I was on the phone with my dad.

"Is she crazy?" He asked Ashley, "It's after midnight."

"We can't exactly stay here," she replied. "Do you have any other ideas?"

He may have, had we given him the chance, but I was already explaining to my half-asleep father that I needed him to come get me, and Mike, and Ashley, and Jody, and bring us back to his small one-bedroom apartment, right now. He didn't hesitate, and it was not the last time I called him in the middle of the night.

By the time he arrived, Mike had told us that the bees were dead. He'd killed them, all of them, by spraying each one, individually, with the mystery chemical he'd repurposed into the carpet cleaner spray bottle. It was safe to leave the bedroom, and we were starting to wonder if we'd called in the cavalry for nothing, if we should just sleep in the house after all. When we opened the bedroom door, a wave of acid entered our lungs, and we hastily gathered sleeping bags and clothes and left the house.

We were waiting on the front steps when Dad arrived ten minutes later, with his new girlfriend, Lin, in the passenger seat. I had met Lin earlier in the summer, when she and Dad had taken me to The Chowder Bowl for dinner by the lake. She seemed nice, and they seemed happy, but I wasn't sure Mike had met her.

Dad sent Mike into the garage in search of the bee-killing, haze-inducing, lung-burning culprit, and I tried to awkwardly introduce someone I barely knew to my best friend, in the middle of the night, feeling guilty and responsible for a situation that no one could have enjoyed, when I suddenly realized how wrong I was. Ashley wasn't upset with me for inviting her to stay at a bee-infested house and having my brother unintentionally spray poison at us. Lin wasn't angry that I ruined her date. My dad wasn't bothered by having to drive across town at one in the morning to rescue us. The dog hopped into the backseat, and I realized we were all just along for the ride, together.

Mike returned with the empty container of rose-spray. The active ingredient was malathion, which Ashley learned years later as a medical student is used as an active ingredient in nerve gas. The directions on the container read: "Dilute one teaspoon into one gallon of water. Spray directly onto rose bushes. For outdoor use only. Do not allow contact with skin or eyes. In case of accidental ingestion, call poison control." Those bees were definitely dead, and the three of us and the dog each claimed a piece of rug and spent the night on Dad's floor. He and Lin closed his bedroom door, and the apartment filled with the sounds of laughter.

Chapter 19
ENLIGHTENMENT FIRE

(John, 21 years old)

1967: "In South Vietnam's national election, General Nguyen Van Thieu wins a four-year term as president with former Premier Nguyen Cao Ky as vice-president. ... There were many allegations of corruption during the election, including charges of ballot rigging, but a favorable impression of the election process was reported by 22 prominent Americans who visited Vietnam as election observers. The Johnson administration cited the elections, held in the midst of war, as evidence that South Vietnam was maturing as a democratic nation."

• *The History Chanel*

Three years out of high school I was learning things I never would have learned in Hopedale, Milford or even Phoenix. The truth of war is different when you are in the middle of it. The only real protection you have is yourself and God's will. You either accept that or you go crazy.

I was in a country where Thieu and Ky had been elected president and vice president in a farce election where anyone who wanted peace wasn't allowed to run, and the winners only got thirty-five percent of the vote. Any kid brought up in Milford would have smelled a fix, but my problem was deeper than worrying about politics or war and peace or who was right or wrong. I was more interested in keeping myself alive.

Pretty much when a soldier got to his final unit he spent his year there and went home. I didn't want to get myself sent to a place even more dangerous than where I was. My mother would be really pissed.

It was undecided whether I would be sent a handful of miles away to an entirely more dangerous situation at Dragon Mountain with the Fourth Division for my year-long tour of duty, or I would stay where I was for the entire tour. I figured if this company was holding three of a kind and needed to draw, it would toss away the chaff in the hand not one of the trips. Determined to be a card they kept, I went to work early every morning, and my headset became part of my body.

Then one morning, just after I had climbed into my chair, put down my coffee and started looking for Radio Australia for some new music, a Morse intercept operator we affectionately called Wop busted into our van. I was the only lingy in this early.

"I have a guy who is going to voice in five minutes. We know his QTH (location) and his freq, but the guy he's linked with is on a different frequency. Can you copy them?"

This would normally need two operators to copy since only one frequency could be called up at a time on the R-390. And I would only be able to tape one of them at a time. I saw a chance to do something that would matter to those making decisions.

"Write down the freqs," I said pushing him a piece of paper and spinning my chair toward the radio.

They were quite a bit apart, but I took a few practice spins on the dial that changed frequencies, figured it would be about two and half spins, clicked on the tape recorder and spun to the first frequency and waited.

"Do you know the other guy's QTH?"

"Yea, he's one of our biggies. He's out by Dak To."

He came up, and as he spoke I typed, but not a normal transcription. Instead I translated it into English. I waited for the radio op to ask for an answer. At "Nghe tot tra loi," (Hear you well, answer) I spun to the next frequency.

I copied both sides of the transmission. They were important, about unit movement. I suddenly became one of the good cards.

That afternoon, Mr. Johns, our W-4 warrant officer, came into the van.

"You Hourihan?"

"Yes."

"Warrant Officer Johns, I hear you're a real wideband receiver."

"What's that?"

"Oh, you haven't been to wideband yet. Come with me."

Within a few dozen steps along the ramp I followed him up three metal steps on the left and inside a van that had no windows. The door opened with a whoosh of air conditioning. It was most likely the only air conditioned room in the central highlands. In the center of the room was the most science fiction machine I had ever seen. Lights flashed and gizmos turned and stopped with precision. There were two ceiling-to-floor, reel-to-reel tape machines with three-foot-diameter reels and five-inch-wide magnetic tape.

Then there was a pos that looked a lot like mine, but with more buttons, sitting at the far end of the room.

Johns motioned me to go sit down.

"Turn that dial to today's date," he said. Now, go to the time that transmission came in this morning." After a few seconds of searching the dials on the face of the machine in front of me I did what he asked.

"Now go to the frequency it was on." He handed me a headset. I put it on and plugged it into the receiver.

I was surprised to hear the same transmission.

"We can do this for how far back?" I asked, looking over my shoulder at him.

"Pretty far."

"We can go back in time and copy stuff we missed?"

He nodded.

"The whole spectrum?"

"Right. We tape everything that is on the airwaves, every frequency, every day, every minute. It's all here." He waved his arm at the contents of the van.

He stopped, "What you did today wasn't necessary." He motioned to me that our visit was over, and as we walked out the door and down the metal stairs to the ramp he added, "But it was never-the-less impressive, and the wideband doesn't translate. Good job."

The next day they sent Mick, a guy I had graduated language school with, to the 374th at Dragon Mountain.

Our company went on 12-on-12-off shifts, seven days a week as the radio traffic got heavier and heavier leading up to November when Dak To, just up the road, and Kontum, even closer, both got hit hard, and knowing where the enemy was became a much more personal thing.

It seemed we were mortared or rocketed nearly every night for a while, and if we weren't at the ops compound we were sitting in a ditch or a bunker waiting for the blackness in front of us to become more meaningful. Spooky dropped illumination flares from time to time to light up the area outside our perimeter, and occasionally it would swoop in and its miniguns would strafe the wood line.

I spent every free moment in the Enlisted Men's Club drinking myself into amnesia. Only my tent mate, Jose Ortiz, kept the stress from melting away our brains like rock salt on ice. Jose was a big man with dark hair and dark eyes and a surprisingly motherly voice. He wanted to be a history teacher. He was probably the most intelligent person in our company where the average level of education was just a little more than two years of college. He was older, twenty-five or so. He was more experienced. He made up history tests, made copies, passed them out, and whoever got the most answers right would get free drinks at the club bought by everyone else who took the test. He was still an E5 buck sergeant at the end of his second enlistment. He didn't expect a promotion soon. He was Puerto Rican.

A few weeks after Mr. Johns had shown me the wideband van, I saw him again. He was walking to the ops compound while I was walking toward the outhouse. You could tell a lot about a guy by how offensive he thought the outhouse was. It didn't really bother me, and I was surprised how many others it didn't bother either. But I thought it was pretty strange that some people got outraged about the state of our latrine. Lots of toilets don't flush, I thought.

I looked up and Warrant Officer Johns was right in front of me. The whole left side of his thin face was a purple mess, his left eye bloodshot, his nose broken and taped. He looked at the ground when he saw me coming.

A few minutes later, inside the EM club, I asked the bartender what had happened, and he leaned over the bar. "He was up on artillery hill at their officer's club, and when he left he got jumped."

"Why?"

"Oh, you didn't know? He's queer."

"What? No he isn't."

"He is. He's a homo … but he's a damn good guy. He's the one who kept Hawkins out of jail for that crap he pulled in the motor pool with the hand grenade. Man, that was funny. I think this whole thing sucks."

By the end of the night, W4 Johns had been avenged. A handful of boys from artillery hill had to go to the hospital in the morning, and their pet boa constrictor was dead.

I saw Johns again a few days later on the same walk. He was holding his head a little higher. As I got just past him I turned.

"Hey, Mr. Johns." He stopped and turned to me. "We know." I paused. "We just don't give a shit. You're one of us, and we take care of our own."

He smiled.

I guess we figured just because someone is different doesn't mean he's wrong.

Johns got the Bronze Star before he left Vietnam, for bravery in the face of the enemy.

Chapter 20
CAJUN SEASONING

(Mandy, 21 years old)

1997: Princess Diana dies in a car accident suffered in a failed attempt to escape the paparazzi, O.J. Simpson is found liable in a civil suit, the N.E. Patriots lost to the Green Bay Packers in Super Bowl XXXI, and Titanic crashes into theaters.

After hitting traffic on the Jersey Turnpike, I exited the Blue Route prepared to embark upon my senior year of college an hour later than planned, and I hate being late. I parked my 1989 black Acura Integra hatchback in one of the three secret spaces next to the Rose Garden, grabbed my Copas and disc from the passenger seat, locked all my belongings inside, and sprinted out to Mertz Lawn to join the middle of the 4:30 pick-up game, already in progress. Most upperclassmen had not yet returned to campus, so the game was full of incoming freshmen and the juniors and seniors who had returned early for their Orientation Committee or Residential Advisor duties. I found my friend, the men's team captain, on the sideline. And after a quick welcome back exchange, we shifted to the season's prospects.

"Looks like a good turnout for both teams."

"It is," he said. "And wait til you see the freshmen you have who played for real in high school."

"Really? That's great! Are they out here today?" I asked, turning back toward the field.

"One is. Look. She's cutting now."

I watched as, with a sharp handler cut, Lindsay left one of the strong returning members of the men's team in the dust. She caught the disc and quickly turned to put up a perfect backhand huck, meeting a receiver in full stride for a point.

I should have been thrilled. We had just graduated the women who had founded our team, who had led our offense and served as our main handlers since its inception. To make matters worse, my co-captain from last year was studying abroad, and as a receiver, my biggest concern over the summer had been who would throw me the disc in the end zone. Strangely, happiness and relief were far from my thoughts. Instead, I felt threatened, defensive. Luckily, I had a solution.

Without hesitation, I sprinted to the other line for the next point, and took my place opposite her, hoping she'd end up marking me, knowing I could put her in her place, prove to her that she was not about to waltz in and be the star. I would shut her down, and I would be on the receiving end of the next point.

I don't remember the outcome of that point, but it couldn't have been pretty. With completely opposite styles of play, we were a terrible match for each other. One quality we share, however, is utter determination, and we each had something to prove, her to the returning team captain, and me, for some bizarre, possibly genetic, reason, to the eighteen-year old freshman.

After several points in opposition, through the nature of subbing into and out of pick-up games, we found ourselves on the same team. The other team had lined up seven men, no women, and while most women would have tried to organize a swap so one woman remained on each team, neither of us was bothered by the prospect of defending the men. A quick turnover gave our team the disc, about ten yards from our offensive end zone, toward the home side of the center of the field. We never exchanged looks, but Lindsay and I both took off at a full sprint before the disc ever touched the ground. She stopped to pick it up, and I never looked back. I sprinted past her, planted about two-thirds of the way deep at the center of the end zone, and cut back toward the front cone on the home side of the field. By the time I looked up, the disc was in the air, with a perfect forehand meeting me in stride at the front cone.

Our enduring friendship began as we exchanged our first of many heartfelt high-fives. Over the next year, we scored most of our points exactly that way, even when the other team knew what we were going to do. I got so confident with our bread-and-butter play that sometimes, just for fun, I stood in the end zone stack and told my defender where I was going to go. It never mattered.

With that game of pick-up, senior year began. It was a year to write the thesis I had researched over the summer, a year to cement friendships three years in the making, a year filled with Ultimate Frisbee, and a year to see new places. It was my last opportunity to live a privileged life in a beautiful place surrounded by truly extraordinary people, and I wasn't going to waste one second of it. In the next twelve months I enjoyed midnight coffee breaks at Paces more often than not, played lacrosse in the halls of Parrish, stayed up all night designing imagined school systems with classmates, wrote my thesis from my single overlooking the Rose Garden, chased lots of Frisbees, and crossed the Mississippi for the first time.

As soon as I returned for my final semester in college, a few of us began looking for new and interesting tournaments. For the last three springs, we had started Spring Break with an eighteen hour drive to Gainesville, Florida to camp at Frostbreaker, and then travelled on to Sarasota, and stopped up the coast for a second tourney. Just as it had for the previous three springs, our college season schedule included trips to Princeton, Penn State, Haverford, Maryland and Rutgers. The day after we searched rec.sport.disc for something different, seven of us crowded the desk of a triple-A travel agent in Philly as she searched for plane tickets and hotels for us in Baton Rouge and New Orleans during Mardi Gras. I charged mine on my brand new, 0%-APR-for-six-months credit card I qualified for after two years of charging team expenses and paying them off monthly on my student card. I don't think any of us bothered to tell our parents about our plans, at least I know I didn't.

We skipped a couple days of classes for the adventure, and I feared telling my beloved advisor that I would miss her seminar. My fears were unfounded, as she simply wished me a fun trip. Our flight connected in Houston, where we tossed a Frisbee from escalator to escalator, squealing about how most of us had just crossed the Mississippi for the first time, and how we were in Texas, of all places. A man in a cowboy hat turned at that statement to explain to us that "y'all aren't in Texas, y'all are in Houston." We exchanged quizzical expressions assuming his ignorance before resuming our Frisbee toss through the airport.

The trip was only five days long, but the memories surpassed those made in any previous month, or possibly even year, of my life. My first trip across the Mississippi also brought my first experience with trash barrels full of Cajun crawdads, my first torn MCL away from home, my first stay in a La Quinta, with a pool we made them open for us in March, my first Expedition rental, which drove through my first drive-through margarita stand, my first Pat O'Brien's Hurricane, my first well-earned Mardi Gras beads, my first trip to the lobby of Louisiana Central lock-up (and second time calling my father in the middle of the night), to a bail bondsman, to the inside of a New Orleans courthouse, where the jackets on the crowd read like a who's-who of Ivy League athletics ("Princeton Rugby," "Yale Football"), my first glimpse of the mouth of the Mississippi River itself, in all its muddy glory, and many, many beer-filled Frisbees shared with total strangers. It was a weekend of extremes, of joy and pain, of excitement and terror. I returned home on crutches and skipped an extra class to sit with Lindsay on a parking lot curb for sixty minutes as fourteen rolls of her film were developed at the local photo shop. I claimed all the doubles, and before allowing ourselves to descend from the high of the trip, we vowed to return the next year.

Chapter 21
IF YOU DON'T LIKE YOUR JOB,
LET THE BUCKET DOWN

(John, 22 years old)

1968: Tet Offensive. "The North Vietnamese Army launched a wave of attacks in the late night hours of 30 January in ... South Vietnam. This early attack did not lead to widespread defensive measures. When the main North Vietnamese operation began the next morning the offensive was countrywide and well coordinated, eventually more than 80,000 North Vietnamese and Viet Cong troops striking more than 100 towns and cities, including 36 of 44 provincial capitals, five of the six autonomous cities, 72 of 245 district towns, and the southern capital. The offensive was the largest military operation conducted by either side up to that point in the war.

The initial attacks stunned the US and South Vietnamese armies and caused them to temporarily lose control of several cities, but they quickly regrouped to beat back the attacks, inflicting massive casualties on North Vietnamese forces. During the Battle of Hué, intense fighting lasted for a month resulting in the destruction of the city by US forces. During their occupation, the North Vietnamese executed thousands of people in the Massacre at Hué. Around the US combat base at Khe Sanh fighting continued for two more months. Although the offensive was a military defeat for the North Vietnamese, it had a profound effect on the US government and

> *shocked the US public, which had been led to believe by its political and military leaders that the NVA were, due to previous defeats, incapable of launching such a massive effort."*

> • *Wikipedia*

When you get the hungries, you get the stupids.

After four months of a driving monsoon rain and the rest of the year in the smoldering furnace of the dry season, I was hungry for wine, women and, well, more wine and more women, and ice, and milk that wasn't reconstituted. I extended my tour in Vietnam six months to get a free thirty-day vacation at home where I expected a uniform would attract women. In this war that wasn't the case. That confused me.

The closest I came was while driving aimlessly around one afternoon in a neighboring town I saw a young girl walking along the side of the road in a yellow bikini. I thought God must have been taking pity on me, so I stopped beside her. She approached the passenger's side of the car and bent to look in the window. My heart nearly stopped. She was beautiful, and although I figured her to be sixteen or seventeen, I threw legalities out the window she was peering in and I asked, "Do you want a ride?"

She thought for a minute and then said, "I am teaching swimming at the lake. I have to go." She smiled and then ran to a dirt side street and bolted toward the town beach. I really thought she was going to get in. She was gone, just like that, but I took an impression of her face with me back to the jungle. She was that beautiful.

When I stepped back into Vietnam, the Tet Offensive of January 1968 was just winding down. It was my absence during the worst time most of my friends here had faced that gave me a reputation for knowing when to get out of town. From then on, every time I put in for a leave or R&R, 50 others did too.

In my return briefing, where I was to be told everything important that happened while I was gone, I found that during the Tet Offensive nearly 38,000 Viet Cong had been killed, a half million civilians had become refugees, and 2,500 GIs had been killed. Khe Sanh was under siege in the north and a linguist would need to be sent to help the Marines and Army still there, Nha Trang and Saigon were both being hit, and we had lost Hue. However, I sat in the Quonset hut and heard, ironically, how the Tet Offensive had been a debacle for the North Vietnamese Army and the Viet Cong who had sustained heavy losses. As an aside, the W4 giving the briefing mentioned that a defoliant called Agent Orange would be sprayed around our perimeter the next Wednesday to kill the vegetation. Jose Ortiz, who had become like a brother to me, was dead. The C-130 aircraft carrying him down country to go home had hit the side of a mountain. It was carrying bombs I was told, and we were going to name the company ball field for him. Oh, and I was to be promoted again.

Only a few days later, when I returned to the ops compound and had stopped at the coffee station half way down the ramp, I saw a commotion at the control van.

As I walked into the crowd, Mr. Johns turned toward me, "One of our sister ships has been captured by the North Koreans."

"Are they all dead?"

"No, it seems the skipper didn't do it. When it looked like they were going to be boarded he locked the MPs in the brig."

We both laughed, knowing that the standing orders on that ship were the same as they were here in Pleiku. If we were to be overrun, the Military Police, our drinking buddies, had orders to kill everyone, using that M-60 machine gun on top of the shack I suppose. "There is just too much knowledge in each person in this outfit, in this situation," I was told once. This fantastic naval leader didn't let it happen.

"What's the name?" a voice behind me asked.

"The Pueblo … It's one of ours (meaning a listening ship … a spy ship.)"

"No, I mean the captain."

"Bucher."

"Well, God bless that skipper," I said. As I turned to leave, Raymond was standing behind me. Raymond was the giant blond MP from our gate. "You bet your ass," he said, and we laughed. His face was puffed and white like bread dough, obviously thinking about what he would do if the time ever came. "God bless Him," he added. It sounded strange because people didn't usually mention God in the war zone … well, not out loud.

No one at home was ever told by our government what the standing orders were for what was to happen to the men on board if they were about to be boarded. Instead, when Bucher was released, having been severely tortured, he was nearly court-martialed, and then spent the rest of his career in obscurity.

I left the group discussing the Pueblo and walked to my van. Every linguist from both shifts was in the van when I got there. They were about to draw lots to see who would be going to Khe Sanh. The forward fire base that was supposed to watch over the Ho Chi Minh Trail as it passed just south of the DMZ had been completely cut off, with all its roads blocked, and was surrounded by NVA soldiers and tanks, it was not a place into which any of us wanted to be choppered.

I was suddenly wondering, for a brief moment, if it might not be so bad to be the one chosen. It would be a great way to jump ahead in rank, but before the drawing could take place, Rat, a Department of Defense special representative, sidled in among us.

Rat earned the nickname because he was only 5-3 and weighed maybe 110 pounds. He had dark hair and a pointed nose and wore Buddy Holly glasses, and he spoke Vietnamese like a native. The high-ranking civilian edged his way through the crowd, and when he got to Isa who was holding the hat with all our names in it, he took the hat, dumped it on the floor, handed it back to Isa and said, "There's no need for that."

No one knew what to think. We had seen this young man walking around the company in civvies, and, beyond wondering why he wasn't in the Army at his age, we didn't think much of him at all.

"I'm a linguist … I get paid more than you guys … It's my job … I'm going." He walked out of the van. He seemed to grow into a giant in the mist as we watched his back walk off down the ramp, into the darkness and straight for the officers' club.

By the end of the Khe Sanh siege and bombardments, two divisions of North Vietnamese Army soldiers had been reportedly decimated and too many marines and soldiers had been killed or wounded.

When Rat got back we talked with him and found out that what was being told to the media was a far cry from the truth of what had actually happened at Khe Sanh.

For instance, it was reported to the public that 10,000 to 15,000 North Vietnamese Army regulars had been killed and 205 Americans.

It all sounded nice in a war where wins were being counted by how many more of the enemy you killed than how many of you the enemy killed in return. Sitting in a Quonset hut in the Central Highlands, those of us who might have gone there if it hadn't been for a young Department of Defense linguist, were told that rather than the staggering 75 to 1 kill ratio being told to the public, the real numbers were probably more like 5 or 6 to 1. Rather than the 15,000 enemy deaths to 205 American deaths reported stateside, the numbers were more like 5,500 NVA killed to just under 1,000 U.S.

Those who fought at Khe Sanh fought an incredibly valiant battle against a much larger army while only being resupplied sporadically by air.

Rat had been choppered in and was stuck inside the fire base when the attacks got hot, and he made it out in June.

In June of 1968, the abandonment of Khe Sanh had begun. It was around the same time as the assassination of anti-war presidential candidate Bobby Kennedy. Khe Sanh was totally empty of U.S. forces by July, when Mayor Daley let loose the Illinois National Guard on young Americans outside the Democratic Convention in Chicago who were protesting the Vietnam War. It seemed to me that in 1968 we Americans were in the habit of wasting lives.

"The Mỹ Lai Massacre ... was the ... mass killing of between 347 and 504 unarmed civilians on March 16, 1968. It was committed by U.S. Army soldiers of the ... 23rd (Americal) Infantry Division. Victims included men, women, children, and infants. Some of the women were gang-raped and their bodies mutilated. Twenty-six soldiers were charged with criminal offenses, but only Lieutenant William Calley Jr., a platoon leader in C Company, was convicted. Found guilty of killing 22 villagers, he was originally given a life sentence, but served only three and a half years under house arrest.

...

The incident prompted global outrage when it became public knowledge in November 1969. The My Lai massacre increased to some extent domestic opposition to the U.S. involvement in the Vietnam War when the scope of killing and cover-up attempts were exposed."

• *Wikipedia*

Something the public also wasn't told, that we found out about later, was that, in March in a place where American soldiers had been killed almost daily since the war had begun, a plan was put in place to put an end to the notorious Vietnamese village of My Lai in an area called "Pinkville" because that was the color it was on the military maps. Snipers, booby traps, mines, rockets, mortars and what the Army believed was a town filled with NVA, VC and VC families had been killing GIs at an alarming rate. Under orders, and with the explanation that they would be allowed to avenge American soldiers who had been killed and to make matters right, a "Search and Destroy" incursion by a company ended in at least 200 civilians being massacred in the village of My Lai. Their mission, their orders, had been to destroy the village and kill the inhabitants. That number varies with each telling, but that was the initial number I heard. Some say the number was closer to 500. Dozens of young soldiers were charged with murder of civilians, even though they had been told that if there were people in that village they were the enemy or enemy sympathizers who had caused or allowed so many dead and wounded, some only a few days earlier, of American soldiers just like themselves. So, a group the same as the soldiers I had seen in the airport terminal years before, 18-year-olds searching the heat haze of war for someone to tell them what to do next, were told what to do, and because they did it they were taken to court. They were trained to do what they were told by anyone of a higher rank, and although the instructions came from much higher up, only one lieutenant was eventually found guilty and sentenced to life in prison. This massacre caused outrage, but few outside Vietnam even knew that thousands were massacred in Hue by the NVA around the same time. Those who were never in war forgot that war is hell. It is not a euphemism. It is actually hell. Our country put these boys in hell and they acted accordingly.

I decided that since killing people could be arbitrarily seen as either heroic or murder after the fact, since the media decided which "massacres" were to be published and which were to be kept in the dark, since we lied about everything both to our soldiers and to our own public, since our allies could be wiped out by our own guns on the say-so of a kid only a month in country, since it was not OK for seventeen and eighteen year old boys stuck in a war to kill people who they had been told were the enemy, but it was standing orders that our own people were to be killed by our own MPs rather than allow them to be captured, since life and death could come down to drawing names out of a hat, and since we lost hundreds of people defending land we would then just abandon, I gave up on the war. I decided that, even after the onslaught of reality, I had some morals left from my upbringing.

The Tet Offensive was called the turning point of the Vietnam War. It was for my country, and it was for me as I realized all may be fair in love, but nothing is fair in war.

Shortly after, on just another siren-wailing alert telling us we were probably going to be mortared or rocketed or attacked in some way, I went to the operations compound without my M14.

"Where is your weapon, Hourihan?" Captain McCollough demanded as I stepped onto the ramp.

"I suppose you have it, sir."

"Damned right I have it." He pushed the rifle toward me.

"You keep it, Captain. I don't want it."

"What are you now, some kind of conscientious objector, some kind of fucking hippie?"

"No," I said and tried to walk past him. He sidestepped and blocked my way.

"This won't get you out of here, you coward."

"I'm not asking to go home, sir. I'll stay here. I'll do my job. I just won't carry that rifle anymore."

"God damn it, what will you do if you meet the enemy?"

"Don't be stupid sir, if I meet the enemy I'll probably lose, since I won't have a gun and he will."

This stunned him. I even thought I saw a hint of a smile.

"Look, captain," I said calmly, trying to soften the situation, "I'm not a coward, ask around. Let's compromise; I am willing to die for my country." His eyebrows raised. "I'm just not willing to kill for it anymore."

This time he let me pass, and I went to work.

From that time forward, it felt as if Vietnam and I had stopped being at war with each other. When our company was to be hit at night, my flak vest and helmet would magically appear on my pillow that afternoon, and once I was approached in the EM Club by the woman we had hired to keep the books.

Tuyet was one of our oldest hirees. She had been here since early '67. She took my arm as the evening turned to dusk and pulled me aside.

"Anh Lua, you have to go to work now." My Vietnamese name since school had been Anh Hanh, but ARVN soldiers I worked with had told me a better name would be Lua, Vietnamese for "fire."

"Too early, Tuyet. I have a few hours left. I'm working mids now."

"You go now," she ordered.

She was an old friend, so for some reason I went to work, and the company area was mortared within minutes. No one was hurt.

I chalked it up to luck. Then a few months later Tuyet got taken away by MPs, and a mess sergeant took over the books at the club. Rumor was that Tuyet had been a captain in the NVA. All I could think of was, "Wow, a woman with five kids held a combat officer position on the other side, and we wouldn't let women fight at all. I guess they want it more than we do."

I would spend about a year and a half more in country doing my job, without a gun. It could, and was, argued that doing my job would kill people. But my job was to let our people know where the enemy was and was not. What they did with the information was their decision, not mine.

But first, when my extension was over, I would spend a few months in Torii Station, Okinawa until by mutual agreement the Army and I realized I was having far too much fun in Koza City and Kadena Circle. I wanted to leave before I ended up in jail, and the Army wanted to oblige.

I really didn't expect they would send me back to Vietnam, but they did. And, of course, I got busted to E4, for the "fun" thing.

Chapter 22
IT'S HOW YOU PLAY THE GAME, OR NOT

(Mandy, 21 years old))

1998: In February Osama bin Laden publishes a fatwa, declaring war against Jews and Crusaders. Matt Drudge, an Internet reporter reports there has been a sexual affair between President Bill Clinton and an intern, Monica Lewinski.

Six weeks after Mardi Gras, Marie and Doug, the school's athletic trainers who were not technically assigned to work with club sports but had gotten to know me all too well, cleared me to return to Frisbee, and I ran directly from the field house to Mertz Lawn. I had stepped down as captain at the start of my final season, hoping to open the door for an underclassman to learn the ropes before I left completely, and to enjoy myself on the field without the added responsibilities of running the team, but I never fully yielded control. I can imagine their frustration as I sprinted onto the field, yelling "Seven on the line," effectively ending the drills they had meticulously been orchestrating. Although I had missed several tournaments, I was back in time for the important ones, and the timing of my return mirrored Lindsay's. Although she had survived Mardi Gras unscathed, a knee injury during our first spring break tournament had sidelined her for a few weeks as well.

Ultimate tournaments are at once pure pain and pure joy. In college, I played just about every point of four or five games each Saturday, followed by up to another four games in elimination rounds on Sunday. We play on the worst patches of grass of any sport, without coaches to tell us to stop, lines to assist in boundary recognition, referees to manage fouls, or trainers to advise us on treatment. The sport requires constant sharp cuts, which wear down your joints, and offers no rest time until the point ends. In any given weekend, we rose in the middle of the night to drive hours away. We ran, jumped, and dove for six or more hours a day, two days in a row, and after it all, we limped off the van on sprained knees and ankles, with concussed heads and skinned bodies, separated shoulders and bruised kidneys, and on a natural high from a weekend in which we played our hearts out with our closest friends, experienced thrilling victories and crushing defeats, cheered our opponents after each game, and left all our cares behind for forty-eight hours, living in a utopian sport governed by "Spirit of the Game," functioning without the intervention of anyone other than the players themselves. With any luck, I would return the van to Budget, and park my Integra on campus by 9:45 p.m., so that I would have time to cash in my meal credit at the snack bar for a pint of Ben & Jerry's before it closed and strategize with teammates about how we could beat UPenn next weekend before I had to return to my studies.

The Mid-Atlantic Region was competitive, led at the time by the North Carolina teams and Rutgers, and with each progressive year, our fledgling team ascended its ranks. By my senior year, we had surpassed many teams, and believed we had a distant chance at qualifying for Nationals for the first time. Regionals began on a beautiful, sunny, April Saturday at Princeton, and in our opening game we scored seven points on the perpetual champion Rutgers' team. Our zone defense slowed their potent offense enough to earn a time cap, and we only lost by a score 10-7. It marked the first time we had scored more than a point against them, as well as my first (and second and third) full lay-out defensive blocks as the short deep in the zone. We were fired up for our next game against the team we viewed as our primary rivals, UPenn. We had never beaten Penn, but we always thought that we could, and we knew we would have to beat them if we wanted to earn a bid to

Nationals. We left our Rutgers game both fired up and exhausted, and lost by one point on a hard-cap to Penn during pool play. We finished Saturday with two easy victories, and entered elimination rounds 2-2.

I awoke Sunday morning to find the return of the 40-degree rain that seemed so common in the Mid-Atlantic, and when I stepped onto the van, only six of my teammates joined me. I turned to the new captains, and they had little to offer in the way of explanation. One was sick, one was hurt, one had too much work, clearly no one wanted this as much as I did. Playing savage, the Ultimate term for without subs, we won our first round game easily, and met UNC in the second rainy round. We escaped the almost fatal error of dropping the pull on their end zone line at dual game point when the wet disc slipped from their hands for the win, and we managed a victory as Lindsay somehow put a huck through the rain with her injured shoulder, meeting my end zone layout grab for the win. Covered head-to-toe in frozen mud, we advanced to the game-to-go to the game-to-go to Nationals.

Unfortunately, during that game, we also suffered many injuries. Among others, our team sported an injured back, a broken thumb, a separated shoulder, and I had sprained both my ankles. I led the team toward the shelter of the van to regroup, and the captain without an injury, sought the tournament director for the details of our next game.

She returned to the van soaking wet, forcing a smile for the team in the back, but flashing a quick pained expression toward the driver's seat for my benefit alone.

"Alright, guys. It looks like our next game starts in fifteen minutes on field four, which is right next to the one we just played on. Wilmington just beat East Carolina in the other side of the bracket. If we win this next one, we'll play Rutgers for the chance to go to Nationals, and we gave them a really good game yesterday." No one looked up or spoke until I broke the silence.

"Who are we playing?"

"Penn."

This was the moment I had worked for my entire college career to achieve. More than anything I had set my mind to in the past, I wanted this battle, and I wanted to win.

I looked back from the driver's seat of the van, and no one made eye contact with me. No one. Our silence was interrupted only by the pounding rain against the metal roof, so strong it seemed capable of denting it as players had by sitting on it during a spring break trip two years earlier. The rain alone spoke for several minutes, until I turned to the captains, who were sitting in the first row behind me.

"Are we going to warm up?"

"I don't know."

I searched the faces of my teammates behind them, and Lindsay finally met my glance from the back of the van, her voice did not convey the pain her eyes revealed.

"If we're going to play, we need to stay loose."

That was it, wasn't it? If we're going to play. It hadn't occurred to me as an option, and I know Lindsay didn't mean it that way, but her words brought our teammates back to life. I allowed for the unthinkable question.

I turned to the captains. "Do you want to forfeit?"

They exchanged glances and looked back at me.

"Only if that's what you want."

I couldn't believe it. Of course I wanted to play. I couldn't walk, but I didn't care. I had half a bottle of Advil left, two Active Ankle braces, and plenty of sports tape, and we were about to play the one team I had always wanted to beat for a chance to go to a tournament I never imagined I'd get to play. And now they were asking me to decide if we play or not? I had stepped down as captain to relinquish this kind of responsibility and just enjoy the end of my college Ultimate career. Or had I?

I collected my breath and turned to my team, their leader for the final time. "Let's go around the van and see how everyone feels. I know we have a lot of injuries," I allowed them.

My friend Gabi went first. She was still only a junior, but had been my co-captain before she studied abroad for the fall semester. She never blinked, and simply, unequivocally spoke up from the middle of the van: "I'm in."

Then I turned to Lindsay in the back of the van, and I saw the determined, fiercely competitive freshman I had worked so hard to beat on the first day of the year, the one who had become one of my closest friends. I knew exactly what she would say.

"I may not be able to throw that well because of my shoulder, but it's Regionals, and it's Penn. We've been working toward this all year. I'm in!" Perfect! And then she added, quietly, to me, "If that's what you want."

With that, the others all fell in line. One by one, their responses mirrored her message. It took three or four versions before I truly heard it: I'm hurt, I'm miserable, I can't play well, but if you want to play, I'll drag myself out of this van into the cold, driving rain, and give it everything I have left and more. The captains went last, deferring to me for the ultimate decision. As much as it hurt, I did what I knew was right.

Without saying a word, I limped gingerly from the van, found the Penn captains I had known for the last four years, explained that we had no subs and several injuries, and that we were forfeiting the game to them. I apologized and congratulated them, and wished them luck against Rutgers. I returned to the van, where Lindsay had gotten out of her spot at the back to move up to shotgun. I turned the key in the ignition, she turned off the radio, and we drove back to Swarthmore with the pouring rain and sloshing puddles as our only music. I parked the van in the field house lot, handed the keys to the captain, and for the first time in years, I didn't return the van to the rental agency myself. Instead, I hobbled slowly across campus to my room overlooking the Rose Garden, closed the door behind me for possibly the first time all year, pulled up my thesis on my computer, and returned to my final edits. An hour or so later, there was a knock on my door, and when I didn't respond, it opened. I didn't look up from my computer.

"Gabi told me about Regionals." I didn't need to look up to recognize the voice.

"How'd you guys do?" I mustered.

"We lost, too. Tough end to our senior seasons."

"We didn't exactly lose."

"Yeah. I heard. I wanted to see how you're doing."

"I'm fine. I'll go to the Training Room and find Marie or Doug in the morning. I'm sure I'll get hell for having played with the first ankle already sprained, but they're used to me by now. I have a lot of work to do on my thesis. I have a deadline on Friday."

"You know you're the only one who meets the deadlines you set for yourself, don't you? It's still early. There's plenty of time. Let's go get some dinner."

I looked up for the first time to the eyes of the person I wanted to talk to more than anyone else at that moment. As the senior captain of the men's team, it seemed he was the only one who could understand how I felt, and I took solace in his concern.

"No thanks. I'm not hungry. I'll see you on the field tomorrow for pick-up."

"You have two sprained ankles."

"Yep."

I turned back to my computer, and after a few minutes of silence, he closed my door and walked away.

Chapter 23
WAR GAMES

(John, 22 years old)

1969: The North Vietnamese peace talks begin. Apollo 11 lands on the moon with three astronauts aboard. Woodstock Music and Art Fair opens in upstate New York. President Nixon authorizes the bombing of Cambodia.

I got so drunk the last night in Okinawa, I woke up in a hotel room in Saigon and had no idea how I got there.

It was more than two years since I had first arrived in country, and my attitude towards what was happening in my life had grown up. I was no longer a 19-year-old child who didn't know his country was at war. The smell of gunpowder, the heart thumping pound of the sound of a helicopter, the sleepless periods, the ghosts of dead friends, the heavy smell of the red clay plateaus, the stink of nuoc mam fish sauce and the skunk-cabbage stench of ba-muoi-ba beer, it all was forever embedded in me. I was a thousand years old, and I finally knew who I was. I was the guy in charge.

It was sun-coming-up early as I lay in a hotel cot snuggled against the relative cool of the plaster wall. I was mostly asleep. I smelled Vietnam, I heard the creak of the ceiling fan, and I felt someone jostling my shoulder. How the hell did I get back here?

I opened my eyes to see white-washed walls and my temporary roommate Blair for the first time. Blair was a stocky reddish-haired Spec 5 with glasses, a white T-shirt and the wide eyes of a new guy. But he didn't look scared like most of them did. It was the white T-shirt that gave him away. Anyone who had been in country for a few weeks had been issued green underwear that wouldn't show up like a neon light in the darkness. Once we were issued the green ones we gave the white ones to any Vietnamese people we came across. At least someone in the states was now issuing them dull green muted unit patches, rank and name tags.

"Let's go. If we don't get to chow pretty soon we won't make the truck," he said. I guess he had noticed that he outranked me, being a Spec-5 to my 4.

"What truck?" I thought of calling him "Nug," something of a derisive name we called new arrivals, short for new guy, but he looked like a good guy so I didn't.

"The truck that brings us to the work details. We have to do that while we are here in Saigon."

"Right," I said sitting up in the bed, rubbing the sleep from my eyes then standing up. "We're not doing that."

We exchanged names, and I found out he was headed to the 330th in Pleiku. I explained to him that E6 and above didn't go to work details. He looked a second time at the E4 patch on my fatigue shirt tossed on the floor beside the cot and stood in wonderment. I pulled two shirts from inside my duffel and threw one to him, and like baptism we were both staff sergeant Benoit. If nothing else, I had learned from past mistakes. If anyone called us on it all we would have to do is run. We were transient. No one knew us, and the name on the shirt pocket tags was of a staff sergeant I didn't like much. He was still in Okinawa. I always hoped he would somehow get in trouble during an inspection for having too few shirts.

It was a test that Blair passed. Without another question, he tore off his own shirt and threw on the new one, and we walked down out of the St. George Hotel into the oven that was Saigon. We went in search of breakfast, walked right past the detail truck and waved.

A few days later, we took a hot and crowded C-123 flight north. Some Vietnamese woman had puked in her hat and held it on her lap sitting right next to me until I took it, walked to the front of the plane, and threw the whole mess out the open window, hat and all. She glared at me for another ten minutes until I turned to her and said one word, "Yee?" It meant "What?"

We stepped onto the tarmac in Nha Trang, and, since I knew the way, we headed straight to the personnel hut at the 313th Battalion HQ. A large stand-up fan was losing a battle with the heat of the dry season, but I stood directly in front of it anyway. It felt familiar.

"Hi," I said to the young clerk at the first desk. "We're headed for the 330th. Do you have our orders yet?"

"Names?"

"Blair George and John Hourihan."

The clerk sat back in his chair and smiled. Which one's Hourihan?"

"I am. Why?"

He stood up and turned to the room of ten or twelve desks behind him and announced, "This is him."

The others just looked up mildly interested.

"Hourihan. This is Hourihan," he explained.

A handful of the personnel clerks stood up and began to applaud.

"Who the fuck are you," Blair asked laughing incredulously.

I thought I had known, but this was a surprise. It wouldn't occur to me for at least another few months that some people in the Army were going to punish me for not wanting to kill anyone. And some were going to applaud.

"What's going on?" I asked the clerk.

"You can't go to the Pleiku. We have orders here signed by a colonel and a general that have requested you not be allowed to return to the 330th. They said you can go anywhere you want in Vietnam but not to Pleiku.

The clerk turned to Blair. "This guy is a legend here. No one has ever been barred from anywhere in Vietnam, especially not by a general." He turned to me and said in a different voice, "Sir, I'll be happy to die for my country, I just won't kill for it anymore." There was more applause and a whistle. This was a part of Vietnam service that no one who hadn't been there would ever understand. Once we had met the people of South Vietnam, heard how they called Ho Chi Minh affectionately Uncle Ho, a lot of us didn't feel the government had made the right choice sending us here, but we felt we owed something to our country. These were the rules, so we showed up and stayed. And by now I had tossed out the thirty years of service idea and was content that the government would pay my way through school if I just earned my money, did my job, stayed out of jail, and got an honorable discharge. Later I would decide that I would only go by other people's rules if they didn't contradict what was right, but for now, I was here.

"So where do you want to go? Saigon, Dalat, You want to stay here?" They were all the best assignments in the country.

"Pleiku," I said. I just had to prod the pit bull one more time. I refused to be dismissed. It was just in my nature.

"But we have orders."

"Hey, how often do you get to piss off a general?" I asked the clerk.

He rolled the orders in a ball and tossed it ceremoniously into the wastebasket.

"Pleiku it is," he said.

In my mind the Army could tell me what time to eat and sleep, but with the help of brothers the Army was no longer in charge.

Chapter 24
DAMN, IT'S GRADUATION

(Mandy, 21 years old)

1998: The Diocese of Dallas pays $23.4 million to nine former altar boys who claim they were sexually abused by a priest. Iraq suspends all cooperation with the UN nuclear weapons inspectors. Impeachment proceedings are begun against President Clinton. In the Security Council of the UN, France, Germany and Russia call for an end to sanctions against Iraq.

I woke up with a pounding headache, and the realization that if I didn't get to Sharples in the next fifteen minutes I'd have to leave campus and spend money for food and coffee commanded me to my feet. On my way out of my dorm room, I stumbled over my drivers' license and credit card, neatly wrapped in a twenty dollar bill, which had clearly been slipped under my door from outside. I shrugged, picked it up, and proceeded to lunch.

In truth, all of senior week remains the glorious blur it was even as I reveled in it. In the weeks between submitting my thesis, completing my exams and graduation ceremonies, I took full advantage of "Camp Swarthmore" and the unique opportunity it offered for stress-free and work-free enjoyment of lifelong friends. I road-tripped to Cape Cod, orchestrated a college-funded "Back to Willets" party for my entire graduating class, passed sober days and altered nights in the Crum Creek and surrounding woods, and, the previous night, strayed with Ashley from the senior class casino trip, opting instead for an evening filled with far too many free Coronas in a local Atlantic City dive bar. We dashed through a downpour back to the casino in time to catch our college-sponsored bus home, and apparently I had lost the contents of my wallet along the way. It was comforting to know that when my thoughtfully constructed plans crumbled, I had surrounded myself with friends who would collect their shattered fragments and return them to me, safely.

And then, the day before graduation, our families arrived, and the world I had confidently created and capably controlled for myself collided with the one that had been shaped for me in my absence.

My mother arrived with my brother, my father with my future step-mother, and we all shared a strained lunch on the lawn outside Sharples. After lunch, broken shoes and family pictures revealed latent animosity and demanded the inception of my perpetual role as referee in a sport that could seriously benefit from Spirit of the Game. Mike abandoned ship, taking the car keys from our mother, promising to return hours later, and Dad and Lin went their own way, as I led my mother on an edgy walk through the magical paths of my life.

Mike returned to claim Mom fifteen minutes before I had to be in line for baccalaureate, giving me plenty of time to run up to my centrally located dorm room to change. The message light on my phone was unexpectedly flashing, and fortuitously I checked it, knowing I could make up the missing time by running.

"Hello. This is a message for Mandy Hourihan. This is Bobby. Bobby Kennedy." My hero since high school had been assassinated almost exactly thirty years earlier, and although my friends knew of my obsession, they could not have known of the crucial timing of their thoughtfulness. "I'm calling to congratulate you on your wonderful career at Swarthmore and to wish you luck in the future."

With a warmed heart and sandals in my hand, I placed the receiver down and ran through Parrish barefoot, across the driveway to the amphitheater, with enough time secure a central spot that had been saved for me, and without time to look around and locate my family, presumably in one or more spots in the audience behind me. Once seated, the guest speaker, Paul Wellstone, delivered his message about inspiration, about making a difference in the world, about using your education for good, and remarkably, about the influence Robert Kennedy had on him as a young, aspiring politician. I exchanged gleeful glances with several dozen knowing friends, reaffirmed in my selection of a college on the eve of my emancipation from it.

Novel challenges about how to enjoy a celebratory dinner in a new family order followed baccalaureate, and I sent everyone back to their respective hotels, finding the prospects of my last package of ramen or the possibility of crashing a friend's family dinner, as preferable options. The ramen ended up in the trash, though, as my advisor overheard my final conversations with my parents and invited me to her house where I enjoyed a peaceful dinner with her husband and children, filled with grilled shrimp and optimistic conversations of my future.

Overnight, another storm brought tornados to the Philadelphia area, but my friends and I remained blissfully unaware as we passed our last soggy night together on campus. Swarthmore was so clearly where I belonged, and to this day, its grounds are home.

The next morning, on Monday, June 1, 1998, I clipped my flower from The Rose Garden and officially graduated from Swarthmore College with a B.A. in my special major of education and history. I haphazardly packed the remains of my room into the Integra, and drove the three hundred miles northeast with my brother to my mother's new condo in Milford, Massachusetts. The following weekend, my mother threw me a huge graduation party, and several Swarthmore friends made the trip to Central Mass for the event. Afterwards, we even managed to convince Mike and his buddies to drink beer out of Frisbees with us.

As soon as the weekend ended, precisely one week after our graduation ceremony, Ashley and I headed west in my dad's Jeep with a roughly outlined AAA U.S. Road Atlas and the Cherokee's compass as a guide on the search for our futures.

Chapter 25
ARE THEY TRYING TO KILL ME?

(John, 23 years old)

1969: President Nixon promises to end the Vietnam War in 1970. On April 5 there is a massive anti-war demonstration in several major American cities. U.S. - North Vietnamese peace talks continue in Paris. Sirhan Sirhan is convicted of killing Robert Kennedy.

I was in Pleiku for a handful of weeks before I realized I wasn't going to be invited back into the operations compound.

There was a little-known trick about Rest and Recuperation leave. You were supposed to get one every six months, and the only thing that kept you from being approved was time in country and if there weren't enough spots on a plane to go where you asked to go. I had only gone once, to Manila, and I had been in country for eighteen or nineteen months.

So I put in for R&R. If they weren't going to let me work, I sure as hell was going to play.

Chuck Roach in the comm center had a list of the empty spots on the R&R roster. A week before I wanted to go I would ask him which destination had empty seats. Thailand was nice. It had empty seats, so I went.

The morning after I returned from Bangkok, I woke up to orders for Phu Bai, and the game was on. This would be only the first gambit in a game in which someone in the outfit would attempt to get me to ask for my weapon back. It seemed I was a "threat to morale" because I didn't want to kill anyone. I just wanted to win the game and go home.

Phu Bai was north of Da Nang, about a mile from Hue, and just short of the DMZ, the defoliated patch between North and South Vietnam. Hue was still under attack, as was Phu Bai. I continued to do my job and made enough friends to keep me from getting into too much trouble, even with their 24-hour horseshoe bar. A visit to Hue as a translator between our operations officer and the ARVN commander who was set up at the Citadel, made my stay less of a problem than they expected. The powers who were involved in Phu Bai decided it was obvious I was going to do my job, even in dangerous situations, even without a weapon and without a complaint.

But it wasn't long before arguments with an idiot redneck buck sergeant about whether or not I would be issued a new rifle helped me decide I had had enough of Phu Bai. But I needed a way out.

I figured since I got myself into this, there must be a way out.

One evening after chow, I twisted the end of a Tareyton cigarette and snapped off the filter so it looked like a joint. I took it out and began smoking it in front of a nug lieutenant who confiscated it and sent it to the Philippines to be tested. I was relieved of duty until it came back. When it came back a few weeks later as tobacco, he was so angry he sent me back to Pleiku, where I joined a rock band called the Inner Union and got to play the Montagnard village of Plei Djrang.

Some Green Berets were stationed there, and they never got any entertainment. When you spend years in a town, even in Vietnam, you make friends, so when a friend, Jimmy Cham, a Montagnard who was battalion commander of the Mike Forces, asked us to play, we played.

After we played rock and roll for a thousand loin-clothed mountain people, I met Neh Bluhm, the village chief. He wore a loin cloth, played every afternoon with the children of the village, spoke seven languages, had addressed the United Nations, and had helped broker the peace treaty between his tribe and the Saigon government just before I had arrived in Vietnam. He thanked us for playing. Then he got us drunk on Montagnard rice wine.

Montagnard rice wine is the foulest drink on the face of the earth. Basically it is rice, banana leaves and meat, buried in the ground in clay pots until river water poured into the pots turns immediately to alcohol. You drink it through a straw.

My friendship with the chief and Jimmy lasted until I left Pleiku. Every time I walked down the dirt road to his village, Jimmy would call out, "Hey, where's your gun?" and I would answer, "Gave it back, Major."

The band continued to play at clubs all over Pleiku for a few months. Our best song was "We Gotta Get Out of This Place." Then on a return trip from playing on Dragon Mountain one night our deuce-and-a-half ended up riddled with bullet holes. We all promptly put in for, and of course were approved for, an R&R to Sydney, Australia.

When I got back to Pleiku, the new trick chief Glen Carney was under the gun with a backlog of tapes of recent intercepts, orders to get them transcribed and sent to Goodfellow Air Force Base in San Angelo, Texas for training purposes, and he had too few linguists to get them done.

Seeking an ally in the game I made a suggestion.

"Get me into ops and let me do them for you," I offered one night while we were drinking at the club. He agreed, and in a week or so I had the backlog finished and up to date and was helping him out on pos.

Because of the work I had done, when two linguists were needed at a detachment called Davis Station II, Mr. Johns and Carney suggested myself and Blair be sent. Our Non Commissioned Officer In Charge was Hambone, a guy I knew from previous years. There were 12 of us at the detachment. I believe it was in a place called An My. The only other U.S. forces there were Long Range Recon Patrols and helicopter pilots and gunners. It was a place where being rocketed and mortared became an every night affair. Sleep became a luxury, and people got killed.

Then one afternoon after an all night mortar attack, we all, including Hambone, got arrested for taking a few dozen cases of beer from behind the LRRP EM Club using the distraction of the attack as a cover. We explained that we "really thought they were ours." We had decided that since the government bought it we were within our rights to take it, since it didn't belong to the Lurps either. The Army didn't see it that way. The Lurps didn't either. They gassed us the next night.

We had done what we came to do. We had set up the detachment, and it could now be run by anyone from our company. We were all replaced and sent back to Pleiku.

Chapter 26
LEARNING THE ROPES

(Mandy, 21 years old)

1998: "Elk Horn, Kentucky: Not to be confused with Elkhorn City, KY. Elk Horn is an unincorporated community in Taylor County, KY. It lies along Route 76 southeast of Campbellsville, the county seat of Taylor County. Its elevation is 735 feet. The origins of the name Elk Horn are unclear: it may be named for a large collection of elk horns displayed at the local mill, or for a pair of antlers found in the area and thought to be unusual."

• *Wikipedia*

With peanut butter and jelly sandwiches on white bread and water from the Nalgenes I had claimed from the end-of-season clean-out of the Ultimate Frisbee lost-and-found, we watched the blazing orange sun dip slowly past the horizon over Lake Erie on Monday night, June 8, 1998, exactly four years before I married a man I had not yet met. Opting to follow Route 20 instead of I-90, we traversed small towns and gently sloping fields adorned with red barns through Western Massachusetts and Upstate New York, spontaneously stopping for a grilled cheese and hot dog at a diner, a mysterious cow with a tag through his ear, and the Seneca Falls plaque commemorating the first Women's Rights' Convention. Our first tent site was securely wedged between two adjacent sites, directly across from the bathroom. For added safety, I made sure to lock the door before we fell asleep by clipping my barrette through both zippers to connect them. My ingenuity was admonished in the morning, however, when it frustrated Ashley in her attempt to make coffee, and she not-so-calmly explained to me that my anti-theft device would not prevent a bear from entering, it would only stall our exit in the case of emergency, caffeine-related or otherwise.

So passed night one of a two-month camping trip that I had embarked upon with just enough experience to not realize I probably should have warned my traveling companion that I really had no idea what the hell I was doing. It's not like I hadn't ever camped, and I even owned the tent we brought. There had been one trip to the Cape when I was a kid, and a second attempt during which rain drove us into a motel. Then there were three Ultimate Frisbee spring break trips with the team, although on one of those trips, Erika had dragged me from a flooded tent by my feet in a 38-degree Gainesville field and demanded I join the team in the bathrooms to avoid hypothermia.

The next week served as my crash course.

On Tuesday, disguised in yellow slickers we walked under Niagara Falls, crossed the Canadian border without needing a passport, camped a few miles outside Toronto, and enjoyed the first installment of our favorite meal of the trip: Tuna Helper. This one tasted especially good, as it was free, thanks to a gift from a friend of Ashley's dad.

On Wednesday, we exited the highway and got hopelessly lost in rural Ontario, finding our way to a campsite in the hamlet of Shakespeare, next to Stratford, thanks only to the Jeep's compass and our persistence in going south until one road ended, and then west until next one's terminus. That night we tried our first and last box of Hamburger Helper.

On Thursday, we spent our remaining $1.42 of Canadian money on a bad gas station pastry, marveled at the abundantly potholed highways boasted by the auto capital of America, and spent the night visiting Gabi at her parent's Oberlin home situated on the comforting familiarity of a liberal arts campus.

On Friday night we realized we really weren't at Swarthmore anymore.

Late in the afternoon heat, after driving south all day, fighting Ohio traffic congestion and construction zones, we eventually selected a campground along Wilson Creek at Green River Lake just outside of Elk Horn, Kentucky, where the Central time zone line jogs northeast to include our night's destination. We chose it solely on the basis that our free AAA guide showed it as free and less than an inch off the interstate. Unfortunately, much of that inch was unpaved. I was driving, hungry, tired, and cranky when, after an hour and a half, we finally located the dirt lot overlooking a field dotted with ancient oaks, and semi-permanent installations of tired RVs and three-room tents. In the middle of it all, a tarp was strung haphazardly between the outstretched limbs of two trees. In the other direction, a field opened to a ditch with a small body of water beyond it that I never investigated. No sites were marked, so we headed for a vacant picnic table, pitched our shiny new L.L. Bean Dome amidst the K-Mart specials, and prepared our gourmet Tuna Helper. After dinner, Ashley and I sat at the picnic table, with our lantern throwing light from its center, writing in our journals. It was only day five of our trip, and it would be the last evening that either of us even pretended to aim to keep our chronicling current. As we wrote, we began to notice the attention of a campground resident, and after exchanging several glances, Ashley's politeness lifted her gaze in acknowledgement. Taking that as an invitation, within seconds, Jimmy sat down next to us.

"Y'all writin' poetry?"

We snickered, and tried to return to our writing, but he was relentless, and our party of two soon expanded to include a six-foot-tall, strong, bald, tattooed nineteen-year-old, with piercing blue eyes pleading his innocence. A few minutes later, his friends appeared with a deck of cards. Jake was a couple years older than Jimmy and just as clean cut, but possibly the slowest-witted person I have ever met. By contrast, Tyler's long, greasy, dirty blonde locks drew attention from his jagged teeth and beady eyes, and he immediately began spinning yarns of his youth in Oklahoma laced with hints toward a drug-induced past, with a validity we never ascertained. Tyler explained, as he dealt the first hand of hearts, that all three were on leave from the local military base for the weekend, and the tarp we had noticed earlier was their only shelter. On this perfect June evening, that seemed trivial. We closed our journals and pushed them aside, partially to be polite, partially to have someone new to talk to, and partially for the pure entertainment of their three-man act.

Jake couldn't figure out the game, and it was easier to play with four than five, so he wandered the grounds while we played, returning five minutes later with a young boy of six or seven by his side.

"He says there's a tornado here," Jake explained as Tyler claimed victory and re-shuffled the deck.

"This isn't a tornado, Jake," Tyler calmly replied as he passed the deck to his left to be cut after shuffling precisely seven times.

"Yes, it is!" Jake grew animated. "His television says it is!" He turned to the child for support.

"You really think he has a television here?" I asked skeptically.

"I do have one," the child answered. "It's over here." He gestured toward a dilapidated RV. "My parents were watching their shows," he continued. "The news broke in with a tornado warning."

And with that news, for the second time in as many weeks, and the second time in our lives, Ashley and I were in the path of a tornado, on this time we were without the protection of our academic institution.

We were only mildly alarmed at first, as the stars shined brightly through the clear sky. The news returned our solitude, as the boys rose to investigate, and we returned to our journals. Our writing was short-lived. First the winds increased, forcing us to brace the pages as we wrote, and when the first drops of rain threatened to smudge our memories we returned the books to the Jeep and joined the crowd that had gathered around the lone electronic device on the grounds. The residents had determined that a tornado was headed directly for us, and as we were never quite sure exactly where we had landed on the map, we had no choice but to trust them.

We quickly discussed our meager options. We could go sit in the Jeep in the parking lot, but we knew a steel cage could not protect us from a tornado. We could attempt to drive out of its path, but the road conditions were poor even in broad daylight, and for all we knew we would just be driving closer into its path in a failed attempt. So as the winds and rains intensified, we resigned ourselves to our tent, relying on its canvas and nylon for protection. After only a few minutes, we heard the boys outside, and wondering why they had not yet sought shelter, we opened a window enough to see them sitting under the picnic table.

"What are you doing?"

"Our tarp blew away."

I zipped the window shut before Ashley could invite them inside.

"We can't just leave them out there!"

"Why not?"

We sat in silence for a minute before Ashley took a different path.

"Didn't Tyler say he's from Oklahoma?"

"Yeah, so?"

"So they have a lot more tornados in Oklahoma than in New England, right?"

"I guess."

"Maybe he knows what to do if it actually comes through here."

And before she could possibly have heard me say "fine," three soaking wet young men had joined the two of us in my four-man tent.

Time slowed to a crawl, as the storm whipped through us. On Tyler's advice, we each sat against one tent pole to brace it from the wind. The roof bowed under the weight of the downpour, and the tent bulged to the northeast, and with each progressive gust we anticipated the inevitable snapping of the poles. I had never been so scared in my life.

Meanwhile, Tyler regaled us with stories of gator wrestling and acid trips, which may or may not have been one and the same, but nonetheless accomplished his goal of distracting us from our fate. He took a break between stories to explain that he was listening for the sound of a train heading straight for us. If he heard that sound, on his call, we would sprint from the tent through the parking lot toward the water, and lie flat in the ditch on its shore. We nodded, taking comfort in the feigned confidence of a troubled stranger. Less than two weeks after claiming our bachelor's degrees from one of the finest institutions in the land, we found ourselves completely dependent on the knowledge of a twenty-five year old recovering addict who had dropped out of an Oklahoma high school.

A loud crackling noise halted the story just before the gator caught him, and Tyler convinced Jake and Jimmy to run outside to check on the structural integrity of our shelter. They returned less than a minute later, wringing out their shirts, having re-clipped the poles to the tent, reporting that, miraculously, nothing had broken.

Eventually, the rains subsided, and Tyler admitted that he had almost told us to run, but during his hesitation the winds had changed. The next morning's newspaper reported tornado touch-downs within half a mile of our site, but we, and our tent, emerged unscathed to assess the damage around us.

A river now divided the grounds, leaving us on the parking lot side and several others separated from their vehicles by rushing water. An eerie calm presided over the park well past midnight, as everyone stepped out in a shared haze of vulnerability, aware that regardless of our differences, we all just lived the same imagined destiny. As we cleared sticks and downed limbs together, someone managed to build a campfire with wood he had wrapped in a tarp, and a cat meowed his way downstream with a crawfish attached to his mouth. We located the boys' tarp high up in a tree, and through our qualms, we welcomed our new friends to share our tent for the night.

I slept with the car keys in my hand inside my sleeping bag, with my face pressed against the window. For the first time, I had no desire to lock the tent from the inside, but I did want to make sure I could escape it. Before we could fall asleep, a fight broke out around the campfire, and we peeked out to see two grown men fighting with broomsticks.

"Ouch! You burned my ass!" One yelled while removing himself from the edge of the fire.

"Yeah, well you knocked out my toof!"

With that, we closed the window on the early morning hours of rural Kentucky. A brief discussion of time zones as we drifted off to sleep granted us an extra hour, but that hour was to be just as quickly stolen from us.

"Nobody move!" The official voices from outside our tent jarred us from an already tentative sleep.

I unzipped the window again to peek out and saw sheriffs with shotguns surrounding the ring of campers. Incredulous, I moved from the window to allow others a silent look.

"What the hell is that?" One sheriff exclaimed to another while pointing his shotgun at the tarp suspended high up in the ancient oaks.

Apparently Jake felt it was a good idea to respond to that question rather than to follow the initial orders, and before we could stop him, he had opened the tent door and stepped outside.

"Freeze! Hands in the air!"

"No, no," he replied in complete oblivion, which seemed to be the only state he possessed. "I just wanted to explain about the tarp. It's mine." He tried to step away from the tent, but couldn't because Tyler had him by the ankle.

"Don't move!" The sheriffs commanded.

"But that's my tarp. You see, there was a tornado, and it blew my tarp away, and then there was this cat with a crawdad, and it meowed, and these two guys with broomsticks, they were fighting, and did you know that in some places it's one time and in other places its another, at the same time?"

I think his idiocy confused them into submission.

"Son, just get back in your tent."

"Yes, sir."

Certain that the entire place was now awake despite the darkness, the sheriffs spoke to everyone.

"Can anyone explain to us what is going on here?"

I could have explained the night's events, but I had no idea what part of the insanity they wanted to know. Someone finally spoke, explaining the fight between the two men, which apparently caused someone to call the police from the payphone next to the overturned port-o-potty.

The men, it turned out, were friends, were intoxicated, and had since passed out in their tent. Neither was upset with the other, despite any missing teeth or burned rear ends. The sheriffs left, and with that, our Kentucky excitement ended.

By the time we woke in the morning and drove off toward Memphis, I had learned that hairclips couldn't protect me while camping, that bears were the least of my worries, and that despite my fancy degree, I had a lot to learn about the world around me.

Chapter 27
A RAGING ANGEL APPEARS IN HELL

(John, twenty-three years old)

1969: South Vietnam: Saigon (Now called Ho Chi Minh City) was the place where most everyone entered Vietnam in 1969. Although it was by no means a safe haven, it was considered about as rear an area as any place in country could be. To move north was considered to be moving to a more dangerous position. The trip from Saigon north to Nha Trang was a 269 mile trek, From Nha Trang to Pleiku was another 189 miles. From Pleiku to Chu Lai was another 164 miles up country, then from Chu Lai to Phu Bai was another 114 miles north. After Phu Bai there was one more city in South Vietnam, Hue, a couple miles up the road. Two other places of note were the Mang Yang Pass and Hon Cong Mountain (Also known as Cong Mountain). Going south east from Pleiku on Highway 19 for about 60 miles, still in the highlands, would be the town of An Khe. In another 50 miles toward the southeast was the coastal town of Qui Nhon. Between An Khe and Qui Nhon was Cong Mountain, and between An Khe and Pleiku was the infamous Mang Yang Pass.

This time it only took two weeks in Pleiku before I was shipped off to Chu Lai, The American Division, where I learned that those who didn't salute officers were sent to the boondocks. This is the division that was responsible for a company of soldiers blindly following orders at My Lai.

I did my job, kept my head down, but when I decided it was time to go back to Pleiku I started using the officers' shower "by accident." The Americal officers couldn't handle that, and I was choppered back home to Pleiku as punishment.

The band continued, but within a month I was sent out to a Landing Zone operated by a "B team" of the 5th Special Forces. I did what I was told, but when I returned from afternoon chow to find an M16, ammo, and three syringes of morphine on my bunk, I went to the commanding officer and explained the situation.

"I'll go out with the platoon. I have no problem with doing my job. I'll carry a radio or something, but I won't carry a weapon," I told him. "Is that OK with you, sir?"

He decided that I had a point, and added that someone with a Top Secret Crypto security clearance shouldn't be out on patrol with a "B" Team of the 5th Special Forces anyways, especially without a weapon. He couldn't figure out how I had ended up in his outfit in the first place, and he allowed me to be choppered back to Pleiku - partially to get the problem off his desk, partially because I was right. Every once in a while you met an intelligent officer.

It had become obvious to me that the idea was to send me to more and more dangerous places until I caved. This became the end of my acceptance of this game. I was tired of the attempt to force me to ask for a weapon.

I had only been back in Pleiku a few days this time before I was sent to Camp Radcliff, south of Pleiku toward the coast in An Khe. Radcliff was a base camp of the 4th Division, and promptly I was shuffled off to their detachment on the very top of Hon Cong Mountain.

There were four Americans on "Cong" Mountain at the time - myself and a nug morse intercept operator in a tent, on a mountain, with one small radio, and two guys manning a quad 50 on the back of a truck.

There was more enemy traffic to intercept than I had ever heard before. It was as if the valley below was a beehive. Then on an afternoon a few weeks after I had arrived, I intercepted a voice message from a Viet Cong unit that stipulated that this mountain that I was sitting on was going to be hit and "occupied" that very night.

I contacted the CQ at Camp Radcliff for a ride down. He said I would have to wait until the morning. There were no trucks available. Then the quad 50 crew was recalled to the valley, and we were there alone. That CQ must have told someone, but we were still up here.

This didn't sound good.

I contacted Radcliff every half hour in the hopes that we would reach a different soldier who would understand who we were up here, and that we knew what was going to happen tonight.

A raging angel, a white guy with a blond afro named Willie Welton, who had been in the CQ office and overheard my plight, took matters into his own hands, "borrowed" an armed personnel carrier, bolted up the side of Cong Mountain and carried us back down to the base camp, even though he had never driven an APC before and had never met either one of us.

The hill was overrun that night, but no one was there.

There was no need to be on the mountain any more so they sent me back to Pleiku.

I heard they took the mountain back a few days later.

Chapter 28
I'LL BE BACK

(Mandy, 21 years old)

1998: The Narrows, Zion National Park: "The Narrows is one of the most unusual hikes on the Colorado Plateau. Hiking is done largely in the river as, for a third of the route, the river runs canyon wall to canyon wall. The walls are vertical and sheer, and often red in color. Water levels change from season to season; most hikers will wade at least waist-deep and many will swim a few short sections. The Narrows can be hiked either as a through-hike from Chamberlain Ranch to the Temple of Sinawava; or as an up-and-back hike from the Temple of Sinawava …

Hiking in the river is strenuous. The water is often murky and the bottom of the river is covered with round, basalt rocks about the size of bowling balls. This makes proper footwear and bringing in trekking poles or a walking stick essential. The Narrows may be closed in the spring due to flooding while the snow melts off the upland areas to the north if the flow rate is higher than 120 cubic feet per second."

• *Wikipedia*

After becoming better acquainted with the Deep South through several communications failures, including one in which I managed to order ketchup cole slaw, we breezed through New Orleans, camped in a hundred degree swamp south of the city, and finally arrived at my cousin Cindy's beautiful home in Houston. I am not sure if I had met Cindy before or not, but I knew her mother well and her grandmother better, and she graciously welcomed us with food, showers, beds, laundry services, tickets to see the Tap Dogs downtown, and directions to local bars and coffee shops. We spent a few days regrouping in Houston, during which we toured the city, the nearby Rice University Village, and took in an IMAX showing of *Everest* at the Natural History Museum. I had been through the Houston airport earlier that year en route to Mardi Gras, but had never stopped in the city. Little did I know at the time that Cindy was introducing us to the home of my future in-laws, a city that would serve as a beloved mid-winter respite for my family for years to come.

With a beautiful cookbook and hand-written directions to the local Jiffy Lube, we left Houston planning to visit the Riverwalk in San Antonio for the afternoon before driving through the night in search of the hot springs of Balmorhea, Texas. Unfortunately, our first colossal miscalculation of distances delivered us to our destination around nine o'clock that evening. We hadn't budgeted for the night's accommodations, so we pulled into a closed campground, pitched our tent illegally, and then broke camp and left before anyone else woke up in the morning. Underwhelmed by the hot springs, which were nothing more than cement walled, open-bottomed warm pools with lots of fish in them, we hit the road pretty early, cutting north at Van Horn toward the Guadalupe Mountains and our first National Park.

Desperate for water, the desert air so quickly stole every ounce from our bread, our peanut butter sandwiches became toast before we could finish eating lunch. That sense of desperation clouded my initial impression of the desert itself. I saw nothing more than charred death and desolation on its grounds. Enjoying only the lone New Mexico oasis we visited, I failed to appreciate the splendor of Roswell or the grandeur of the lava beds we shared with no one, our tent perched alone on an exposed windy mountain. As we crossed the border to Colorado, the grass instantly turned green, and I asked aloud how the weather knew to obey state lines.

"Irrigation."

"Oh."

So the weather didn't know the political boundaries after all, but rather people's values and choices dictated the future of the environment. One knew what was important, the other did not. Or was it the other way around?

We ate ramen with peas for dinner and camped in the cool, dry, Colorado mountain air just north of Durango, where the peaks were still white from the past winter's gifts. On our morning's visit to a frigid lake we met an old golden retriever with whom I did not want to part. After a quick trip to Mesa Verde we left Colorado to the west, just skirting the mountains that hold Ouray, a mountain community integral to my then future husband's childhood.

Up, across, and through Utah, the dryness returned until my heels cracked and bled. We shared what we soon learned were fake beers over a campfire with a couple girls who had just graduated from a Midwestern college and were on a similar adventure, we splurged for a donkey ride on the cliffs of Bryce Canyon, and finally, we made it to Zion National Park where the desert air meets the abundance of the mountains, and a river carves a deep swath through sandstone walls.

I could walk, I could run, I could sprint, jump and dive up and down an athletic field, but I had never in my life gone on anything one would call a hike. That was for a certain group of people, who were clearly not like me. Ashley grew up hiking in the Maine wilderness, and when we had planned a cross-country camping trip with stops in National Parks, she had assumed that was part of the plan. I suppose that was logical, but it honestly hadn't occurred to me.

We found a campsite inside the park, and then left it again to buy pints of Ben & Jerry's for dinner at the local store: New York Super Fudge Chunk for her, Phish Food for me.

As we ate, we pored over the park maps to plan the next day, and deer, so accustomed to people, walked right up to our picnic table to beg for crumbs. For the first time, those deer demonstrated to me the failure of our balancing act between increasing accessibility for all and protecting the natural resources of our land, a point Ashley had been attempting to explain to me for several hundred miles.

The next morning we embarked upon the Angel's Landing hike, rated as the most challenging in the park. I took a picture at the end of each of the first seven switchbacks known as "Walter's Wiggles" before realizing what was going on, and then my boredom drove me to jog up the rest of them. At the top I met chains, anchored into the rock, and I was too young and inexperienced to be concerned as I surmounted them to my first vista point on the top of the world. Brilliant green mountains surrounded us, and an endless valley lay below. It is a scene not unlike many I have glimpsed since then, but it was the first time in my life I had climbed a mountain to earn it, and thus it is one I will always remember.

That afternoon we visited the most well-known spot in Zion. After slicing through 2000 foot sandstone cliffs known as The Narrows, the Virgin River passes through the more heavily visited portion of the park itself at a location wrought with tourists. Ashley hiked up the river a bit to escape the crowds, but I whined, yielded to my weak knees and balance, and after much effort, made it across to the less populated bank. I sat on a rock, allowing the rushing river to wash clarity into my mind, before struggling to find an easier way back. I found none, and complained loudly through my return trip. Despite my protests at the time, the power of the raging river of Zion, much like the enormity of its mountains, left an indelible mark in my mind, and I returned to them only two years later.

We drove from Zion to Las Vegas for a culture shock like none other I could imagine. Only a couple hours apart, they could not be more different. A night of shows, amusement parks, the Circus Circus hotel and chicken-fried steak was all we could handle, so we set off the next afternoon expecting to arrive at a friend's house in Fresno, California two hours later for dinner. Luckily, when we called her from the gas station's pay phone to explain, the skepticism in her voice conveyed the fact that she did not expect to see us so soon.

We sat in a traffic jam for the next four hours, and had dinner at The Original Bun Boy Restaurant in Baker, California, home of the world's largest thermometer: 134 feet tall to commemorate the record-setting 134 degree day in nearby Death Valley in 1913, the year in which both my grandfathers, Bruno and Scrapper Jack, were born.

Then we almost ran out of gas in Death Valley.

But we didn't. Instead we made it to Fresno a little after midnight, and apologized for our late arrival, stayed only the morning, and left for the Bay Area that afternoon.

Finally, on the evening of June 26th, 1998, we emerged from the desert, through a stop in Zion and the insanity of Las Vegas, to the first glimpse of a place I would ultimately consider my true home, and my nagging desire to continually put miles into the rearview mirror halted. We spent the weekend in Berkeley with our friend who had recently arrived to start a doctorate program in physics, visited a few Ultimate friends at Berkeley's International House, enjoyed the San Francisco Pride Parade by mistake, took a detour to visit friends in Silicon Valley, and while taking Highway 1 south to Monterey and driving the Seventeen-Mile Drive around Pebble Beach, watched as the sheer cliffs guarded the vast Pacific from the pavement, and the fog obfuscated its terminus. We had reached the West Coast, in all its glory, and we stayed in the Bay Area longer than we had planned.

When we finally did leave, we meandered through redwoods up The 1, spending several more nights along the Pacific Coast, driving through enormous trees and absorbing its beauty. It was a place to which we both seemed to know we would return.

Chapter 29
VIETNAM PEACE TALKS

(John, 23-24 years old)

1969-1970: Mang Yang Pass: Situated between the Central Highlands city of Pleiku and the small town of An Khe, 50 miles to its east, was the Mang Yang Pass, the site of the last battle of the prior Vietnam war, the one against the French, and one of the bloodiest. At the Mang Yang Pass the French were ambushed by the Viet Minh. The French suffered 500 killed, 600 wounded and 800 captured.

In the next set of orders, the ones waiting for me when I returned from Radcliff, I faced a seemingly unwinnable situation.

Some of the officers involved even admitted to me that I wasn't paranoid, that it was being done on purpose. It seems there were a lot of bets on whether or not I could be "talked into" asking for, or better still begging for, a weapon. Some career Army NCOs and officers seemed insulted that I would turn in my weapon and not even ask to leave the country. It became a concerted effort to make me do just that, beg for a weapon or beg to go home. The longer I avoided what they wanted, the more they saw me as "winning." I had to be very careful because no one plays nice when they are losing.

But as Woody and Scrapper Jack always said, "Deal me your hardest hand and I'll win this goddamn game."

My intent was to not carry a weapon, continue to do my job, pay my debt to my country, stay out of jail, and get an honorable discharge.

The new papers ordered me to be a classified courier for a month. That meant I would rise every morning and get on a C-130 or a C-123, both airplanes I had been told had no explainable right to stay aloft. They were supposedly too heavy for the wing span and power. These were the birds I would climb onto each day and carry 50 to 150 pounds of classified material from one agency post to another.

I was starting to rethink my insistence to be returned to Pleiku. Angry pit bulls, I remembered from Phoenix, could be a real pain in the ass.

There was a hidden catch to these orders, and as I read them a second time I saw what it was.

To do this I needed to have a Top Secret Crypto security clearance, which was OK, and I needed to carry a weapon. Cute.

If I didn't carry a weapon I could be court-martialed for disobeying orders.

On the first day of my new duty, I showed up at the orderly room, as my old man used to say, "Bright eyed and bushy tailed," with a shiny .38 caliber pistol, in a leather shoulder holster, both of which I got from the local national I had hired while I was on house girl duty a few months back. Binh worked in the supply tent, most of the time alone, while his boss "had lunch" at the NCO Club. I wouldn't explain the situation until I returned a month later.

I had met the requirements. I shouldered the duffel bag full of high level classified "code-word" documents and was Jeeped, against my wishes, to the airport.

Every day that month I would do the same thing at some airport. I would jump on a plane, fly to the most out of the way LZs and jump back on a helicopter or a Hercules in the morning to go to the next stop.

Cam Ranh Bay was an enlightening stop, about halfway through my month. I was sleeping on the asphalt lot outside the front of the airport terminal, using all that secret stuff for a pillow when someone kicked my boot.

Standing over me was Buck Sergeant Rick Richards, an old friend from Chu Lai. He was returning from R&R.

"Hungry?" he asked.

I was.

"They are selling chili at the sandwich truck down the street."

I turned to a young PFC with a white T-shirt showing at the neck of his pressed jungle fatigues.

"Hey, nug," I said to him. "This bag is full of classified material. I need you to guard it. I'll be back in about a half hour." I handed him the .38. "If anyone even looks like he's going to try to get near this stuff, you shoot him. Got it?"

He didn't answer, but he took the pistol in his clammy hands and stood in front of the clump of secrets stuffed into a green canvas bag.

As we walked toward the street, Richards asked matter of factly, "Do ya think that was a good idea, telling him to shoot whoever gets near him?"

"Sure," I said. Then after few steps, "The gun's broken … doesn't have a firing pin. It won't fire. Long story."

When we got to the chili truck I examined the long line then went to a point a few people from the chili and stepped in front of a chaplain.

"Forgive me father, for I know not what I do," I said, and smiled the craziest wide eyed smile I could muster. My unconscious mind heard his unconscious mind praying.

My month flew me to LZ Mary Lou, LZ Uplift, LZ English, LZ Bayonet, Da Nang, Phu Bai, An Khe, Qui Nhon, Saigon, Chu Lai, Pleiku, Phan Thiet, An My, Kontum, Dragon Mountain, Cam Ranh Bay, Nha Trang and a few places that didn't have names.

When the month ended, myself and Willie, who had been reassigned to the 330[th,] were promptly sent on a convoy to Qui Nhon on the coast to pick up two pallets of beer. I was the shotgun, without a weapon.

Since I couldn't use the broken pistol again, in a stroke of genius, I had taken an eye test on a two-day layover in Nha Trang, and the 20/400 vision in my right eye said I should not be allowed to "operate machinery or carry a weapon." There was nothing in the convoy orders, however, about carrying a weapon. I guess they just assumed I would decide it was a good idea. I surprised them, and I now had the paperwork to back it up.

We staged with the convoy on Route 19, just to the east of Pleiku city where the shops ended and the plateau extended toward An Khe, then Willie sprinted our deuce-and-a-half out in front and left the convoy behind. Ambushes seldom were sprung on a lone empty truck when an entire juicy convoy was only a mile behind it. We were in the safest spot in the line.

We careened down the edge of the plateau into An Khe, about half the distance to Qui Nhon. We stopped for a few beers at a roadside stand then pushed on to the coastal plain and Qui Nhon city. This was our own detachment, so it was fun reacquainting with old friends, and by reacquainting I mean friendship, steak, eggs and Tiger beer direct from Korea. We mixed it with tomato juice to cut the taste.

The truck was loaded while we slept, and that afternoon we headed back into the heart-stopping, breath-holding, precarious mountain roads and home.

When we entered the orderly room at the 330th we faced Captain Crawler, one of those surprisingly stupid people who had somehow become an officer. He was sitting erect at the center desk and poring over papers.

"Hello sir, we're back."

"So?" he said hardly looking up from his paperwork.

"So, … We need some help unloading the truck."

"What's on it?"

"Two pallets of beer … 120 cases each."

He looked up, thought for a moment then said, "You two do it." And he stood up and walked out of the room.

Silently we nodded and returned to the truck with one thing in mind.

Willie jumped in behind the wheel, and I dove into the shotgun seat, and we left the 330th, and Pleiku, and headed back down Route 19 alone, headed for Qui Nhon … to return the beer.

In Qui Nhon we couldn't find anyone to take the beer back without paperwork, so we changed to Plan B. Driving back and forth, Qui Nhon to Pleiku, and drinking all 240 cases of beer. We didn't really think it through, and maybe we had an overly positive opinion of our drinking abilities, but it was a plan and it sufficed.

"Some plans aren't meant to work," Willie pontificated.

In An Khe, a small village about half way between Pleiku and the coast, we pulled the truck over and walked down the side of the dirt street opposite the side with the open sewage ditch. We stopped at a Ba-Moui-Ba stand just past an open air fruit market. The smell of the fruit and beer mingled with the smell of the benjo ditch. After a quick beer with a green and salted mango, we pushed on to our detachment, a few miles down the road. After I had spent an hour at the club at the det, Willie hustled in and said he had been told that Crawler knew where we were and was going to order us arrested here and sent back to Pleiku, so we jumped in the truck and headed back to Qui Nhon.

In the city we sort of hid the truck behind a Lambretta and a Vietnamese 3/4-ton pickup truck on a side street and got rooms at a hotel overlooking the water.

A girl followed me to my room, but before I could find out why, there was a knock. I answered to two MPs a QC (Quan Canh - Vietnamese for MP) and Willie.

We were under arrest for being in an off-limits city. The MPs staged a convoy with all the soldiers they had rounded up in bars and hotels, and told us we were going to go back to Camp Granite, all we had to wait for was a second MP jeep to lead the way.

After about twenty minutes of waiting, Willie walked to the back of the seven-truck convoy of fugitives. When he returned he explained as he got into the driver's seat and fired up the diesel. "I told him I knew the way to Camp Granite and I'd lead the way."

I laughed.

"Hope they can keep up," he said and popped the clutch into the night.

Welton drove a Deuce-and-a-half truck the way most people drive an MG. After reaching fifty on the narrow streets of the city and a few hard leaning lefts and rights with half the wheels in the air, then a sprint along the coast road, there was no one left behind us, so we went back to the hotel. What the hell, we had already paid for the rooms.

A few hours later we were arrested again. We were ushered to Granite, parked outside the ops compound, and told to stay there for the night. The MP told us that our Commanding Officer had sent an officer and six armed guards to collect us.

We slept in the truck bed, and at first light, we left.

About half-way between An Khe and Pleiku we saw the three-quarter-ton with one of our captains in the passenger seat. In the back were, unbelievably, six armed guards, who all waved to us as we drove right by them going in the opposite direction. None of them bothered to bend over to the window and tell anyone in the front seat.

Our luck ran out on the Mang Yang pass.

Ironically, this was the location of the last battle of the first Indochina War in the 1950s where the French lost several hundred men.

On the left side of us, the mountain climbed straight up, a beautiful plush green overgrown wall with what appeared from the truck cab to have no top. On the right side it dropped down, just as plush and almost as steep.

And in the middle was our truck with a burned out clutch, sitting within a mile of the graves of hundreds of French soldiers who were killed here in the battle of the Mang Yang Pass.

We sat, smoked, and drank for about an hour, refusing to be towed or pushed or driven to Pleiku, just enjoying the freedom from the war, looking out over the greenery that was being fed by the blood and bodies of French soldiers, guys just like us who were just trying to get to Pleiku without getting killed.

At dusk we began to realize the situation we were in was not a good one. Anyone who had been in this country for more than a month knew the night didn't belong to us.

"Did you hear that?" Willie asked suddenly.

I listened for what seemed a long time, and just as I was about to give up I heard it. A rustling in the thick darkening landscape to our right. It sounded like movement about twenty yards off. Then it came again, but in two locations, again, and again, it became a steady movement, and was unmistakably, human or animal moving through the thicket toward us.

"And you didn't bring a gun, nice." Willie scolded as he reached for his M14 and clicked it onto full auto.

"I have something better." I crawled into the back, took a wide stance on top of one of the pallets and started throwing individual cans of beer into the thick undergrowth and shouting "Dung Ban! Xin Loi, Dung ban!" Each time I threw a beer I shouted it again "Dung ban!"

"What the hell are you saying?" Willie demanded.

"Leave that gun alone I'm negotiating," I cautioned, nodding toward his weapon. "I'm saying 'Don't shoot'."

Then we heard it. It was the most wonderful sound I ever heard in Vietnam.

Laughter. There was laughter in the trees and the sound of beers being opened.

Then, after I had thrown nearly a case into our defense, there came one voice.

"Cam on anh," then more laughter.

"What was that?" Willie asked.

"He said 'Thank you.'"

About a half-hour later, before total darkness could set in, the three-quarter-ton pickup truck from our company showed up, and we were carried home to be restricted to our barracks "until further notice."

Willie was told he was going to have to pay for the truck, but they changed their mind when they realized he only had three days left in the Army and when the motor pool sergeant who had been with me at Davis Station II lied and said the truck had a bad clutch when it left.

I had nineteen days left until my original Estimated Time of Separation. But it would be extended.

Chapter 30
THE ENDS OF THE EARTH

(Mandy, 21 years old)

1998: Hyder, Alaska: Originally named "Portland City" in 1907 the Alaskan mining town was renamed for a Canadian geologist in 1914 after the post office reported that there were too many American Portlands. In 1965, just after a camp was established to hold 140 miners with four bunkhouses, a dining hall, recreation hall, auditorium, offices, powerhouse, and a runway, in an area with some of the heaviest snowfall on earth, averaging 800 inches per year. A record sixteen feet of snow fell during the second week of February, and on the 18th of the month, an avalanche wiped out the mining town, and disconnected Hyder's road access to any other points in Alaska. Today, tourists come to Hyder for grizzlies and glaciers, and to get "Hyderized" by drinking a shot of Everclear. On July of 2000, a rare, predatory 300 pound brown bear killed and partially ate a camper at Hyder's Run Amuck campground, three miles from a bear-viewing area operated by the U.S. Forest Service."

Along Highway 101 in southwestern Oregon we saw a sign for Misty Meadow Jams. It was time to switch drivers, so we stopped. With a budget so tight that we were living on peanut butter and jelly and ramen and sneaking into campgrounds after closing and fleeing with the first melodies of daybreak to avoid even their meager fees, I perused the jam selection in the same way I had shopped in every gift shop and tourist trap; it offered a break from the road, but I had no intention of making a purchase. As Ashley headed back toward the car, a label caught my eye: Black Raspberry Jam. I had not sampled its sweetness since that day, thirteen years before, when we scraped the last morsels from my dad's final jar. I threw the $7.00 at the cashier without thinking, and ran back to the Jeep with a newfound energy.

Driving the next shift, I returned Billy Joel's *Complete Hits* to the tape deck, despite Ashley's protests. As her thoughts drifted out the passenger window, my mind wandered to the future. We had just graduated from one of the best and most demanding colleges in the country, one that introduced me to a world of people just like me, who would dedicate their lives to fixing the world, at any cost. I was aware of endless problems in the world, and I wanted to learn more, to solve them all, but at that moment none of that mattered. Instead, as I imagined the next year of my life, I saw Ashley and me sitting at opposite sides of a kitchen table in a city apartment. After waking up late, we were sharing a leisurely breakfast of coffee and black raspberry jam on toast and reading the Sunday paper. The world would have to wait, because at that moment, I couldn't imagine anything better.

The next day, after a festival in Portland, we slept in the Jeep at a highway rest stop to save enough money to see *The Truman Show* in a theater outside of town. Then we drove to Seattle, and we spent the Fourth of July with our roommate and friend who had salvaged my sanity throughout senior year as we shared passionate concerns over social inequalities and life in general over nightly coffee breaks at Paces. I had looked forward to this visit since leaving campus, and we stayed for several days. When we were ready to leave Seattle, her family recommended Vancouver, and since it was only a few hours away, we followed their suggestion. After spending a day wandering around the city, we left without a destination, just in time to hit rush hour traffic.

"What's in the other direction?"

"What do you mean?"

"I mean, we're not moving at all, and there's no traffic going the other way. If we turn around, where could we go?"

Ashley opened the giant road atlas across her lap, turning the worn pages carefully, she settled on the global page, the only one that showed Canada and joked, "We're almost sort of near Russia."

Very funny, but I hadn't been joking.

"No, seriously."

"Well, we're *kind* of close to Siberia."

"No, we're not."

"I guess we could go to Alaska."

"Is it the other direction on this road?"

"Yeah, it is."

"How far is it?" I don't know why I even asked, as these were the days before our iPhones could use Google Maps to determine travel times with and without current traffic conditions, and we had proven woefully incapable of estimating times with our trusty AAA road atlas.

"I don't know. There's a little town on here called Hyder that's pretty far south. I think we could get there tomorrow."

I took the next exit, and we stopped to stock up on Ramen, fill the gas tank, and change more dollars into Canadian currency, before pulling back onto the highway heading north, delaying the setting sun.

We drove for the better part of the next twenty-eight hours, excepting for one short delay when we were pulled over for the second time for speeding. The first had been at dusk in Texas, where we had been driving over the night-time, but below the day-time speed limit, and were issued a warning for, as far as we could figure, driving with northern plates in the state of Texas.

"License and registration, please," the polite Canadian officer began.

Ashley handed over her Maine license, and I produced my dad's expired Massachusetts registration from the glove box. Then we smiled innocently at the officer's grimace as he perused both documents, presumably comparing names, states, and dates, before handing them back to us through the open window.

"I don't want to deal with this tonight. Just go, and please slow down."

We crossed the border from Stewart, British Columbia to Hyder, Alaska at an hour that would have been dark in any other state in the union. A "Welcome to Hyder" banner stretched across the road as it turned to dirt, a condition it would maintain throughout the town, and vacant booths capable of holding customs officers bookended the road. We took photos and drove on in case darkness caught us eventually. Hyder, Alaska is home to not much, but it did have a campground. We paid for a site, selected one with no neighbors since, despite the abundance of bears in the region, I no longer sought solace in the proximity of intimate strangers, pitched our tent, and slept through a night whose sky grew dim, but never achieved total blackness.

When I emerged in the morning, a new tent had been planted next to ours. It was not staked out, and its owners had failed to clip the poles to the bottom, so it scrunched up the poles forming a round, structurally unsound mass.

"Who the hell put that up?" I asked Ashley before noticing that she was sharing coffee with a man.

"I did."

Oops. At that point what was the harm in continuing? "Well you didn't do it right."

"I know. It was late. Do you want some coffee?"

"Sure. Who are you? And why are you at our picnic table?"

"My friend packed the stove and coffee. We got in late and he's still asleep and I don't know where he put it. Your friend was kind enough to share."

Of course she was.

I, on the other hand, am always grumpy and anything but sociable before coffee. Perhaps that's the reason she was happy for the pleasant company. It turned out that Bill was 30-something, and he and his friend, Mark, were old friends. They lived in different places now and only saw each other once a year, when they left their families at home for the weekend and planned a trip to spend some time together. It all seemed peculiar to me. Why would old people camp? Why would you live far apart from people you cared to see? Why wouldn't you make the time to see them regularly if they mattered to you? And why wouldn't you just take the whole family? By the time Bill handed me my morning coffee, I had decided that he was a strange old man, whom I would never understand. It wasn't until fifteen years later when I was flying home from a backpacking trip with Ashley that I realized he wasn't so different from me after all.

When Mark woke up, they took their tent down quickly and left while we were relaxing with our second and third cups of coffee, searching our inadequate Alaska map for a plan. We had arrived in Alaska, now what?

With no other ideas, we broke camp and followed the only street on our map, a dirt road which only went about a millimeter beyond the campground. We planned to follow it until it ended and then reevaluate, but as we drove down it we were surprised by the realization that cars were passing us in the other direction. Long after we had expected it to end, we came upon about a dozen cars parked along both sides of the road. After parking at the end of the line and getting out of the Jeep we were immediately commanded to silence by the people we had not yet noticed standing on the other side of a thin row of trees. Obediently, we traversed toward them, and were silently greeted by a ranger.

"What's going on?" I began a hushed conversation.

"The grizzly's over there, fishing for salmon," she pointed beyond the tourists to the bridge we had yet to notice, where a stream flowed freely. "They're here to watch."

"Why are you here?"

"I'm stationed here with a stun gun. If the grizzly notices the people and approaches, I'm supposed to shoot."

This was clearly not the assignment she had imagined when joining the National Forest Service.

"The bear or the tourists?"

She laughed. "So, y'all are here to see the glacier?"

"Um, what glacier?"

"No?" Her eyes remained fixed to the grizzly as she spoke. "If you're not here to see the glacier, then why are you here?"

We stifled our giggles. "What is this glacier?"

"The Salmon Glacier. It's about seventeen miles up the road."

With no alternate plans on one hand, and hesitation about venturing seventeen miles down an untraveled dirt mountain road on the other, we exchanged shrugs before our discussion was pre-empted.

"You should definitely go," we turned to find Bill and Mark had been standing behind us for an unknown length of time.

"I'm not sure it's the best idea."

"Why? What kind of car are you driving?"

"A Jeep Cherokee."

"That's what we're driving, too. It has four-wheel drive. You'll be fine."

When we didn't respond, Bill filled the void.

"You know what? We'll go with you. That way you won't have to worry about getting stranded if anything happens to your car."

The bear left and the ranger returned to the conversation, presumably believing we knew these men from more than just our morning coffee. "It's really quite stunning. It's one of the largest glaciers on the continent."

I don't remember either of us making the decision, but the next thing I knew we were taking a seventeen-mile drive up a windy, washed out, dusty mountain road toward the promise of a large sheet of ice, with two old men we had just met following behind to keep us safe.

An hour and a half later we pulled into an established overlook point, parked the Jeep, waited for the men to follow suit, and got out for a better view. Through the overgrown trees, a rocky embankment channeled an angry river. At least twenty yards wide, its frigid waters escaped the edges of the glacier, which had receded into the distance to our right. The road we had followed did not end, but rather it continued in the direction of the glacier itself.

"Do you think this is really the vista point?" I asked anyone who would respond.

"I don't know," Mark answered first.

"According to the odometer, we've gone seventeen miles," Ashley added. "And this is clearly an area that was once meant for cars to pull out. The glacier is probably just smaller than it used to be."

"I guess," Bill offered, "but the road keeps going. We've already gone this far. Maybe we'll get a better view if we keep going just up past the hill there."

With an hour and a half already lost for a glimpse of the gray-blue edges of an icy slope, and still no other plans for the day, we returned to the Jeep.

"I don't like this at all!" Ashley barked as she pulled out behind them.

"What?"

"We were too slow getting into the car and now we're stuck eating their dust."

Ashley knew so much more about driving on dirt roads than I did, but at least at this point I had learned that I should let her do the driving on them or we would never get anywhere.

"Oh, that's all?"

"Yeah, what did you think I meant?"

"I don't know. I was starting to wonder if this is a good idea."

"Yeah," she admitted. "One of those guys is starting to remind me of someone, and I can't place who it is."

"Me, too! Mark, right? It's been bugging me all morning. I noticed it at the campground."

"Do you think we've met him before?"

"No."

The conversation waned, and I turned the volume up on the radio. Music had been a battle for weeks, with my Billy Joel obsession driving Ashley crazy and her U2 cassette deriving similar responses from me, but Simon & Garfunkel's *Concert in Central Park* served as an amicable middle ground. With the windows up to keep the cloud of dirt at bay, their voices provided cover and distraction, until the suggestion of spies on a bus while searching for *America* reminded us of our suspicions.

The Edge of Paranoia

"I think he reminds me of someone from a movie. Does he look like an actor?"

"I'm not sure. What movie?"

"I don't know," I tried to freeze the image in my mind before its tentacles released their fleeting grip and slipped away completely. "Maybe a horror movie?"

"Maybe."

"I was kind of thinking maybe we shouldn't be following them."

"Yeah, me too."

"What if he's not from a horror movie, but we saw his picture on the news or something."

"Do you think?"

"Not really, but could be."

"They did seem awfully eager to get us to go to the glacier this morning."

"Yeah, and where did they even come from when we were watching the grizzly? I had no idea they were behind us."

"And do you think it was almost like they knew where they were going when we stopped after seventeen miles and they wanted to continue? Like they've been here before or something?"

"Yeah! I noticed that, too."

"So what do we do?"

"Should we turn around?"

"Yeah, but won't they notice?"

"I guess, and we're already hours away from any other people, down a barely passable mountain road."

"So we should probably just keep going, right?"

"I guess. This road has to end eventually."

It had been at least an hour since we'd stopped, and almost that long since we had seen any hints of the glacier, when the road in front of us ended, and the men slowed down and stopped their car in the middle of the road. We pulled up along their left, and I opened the passenger side window. Ashley kept the engine running, just in case.

"Now, what?" Bill asked from the driver's seat.

"I don't know. I guess we have to turn around and head back."

"Yeah. Unless …" he hesitated, and Mark picked up where he left off.

"Look!" Mark pointed through our Jeep to a hint of an opening between trees. Possibly having once been a road, it was now hopelessly overgrown, yet still passable.

"You want to go there?!" We asked in unison.

"I don't know," Bill started reluctantly. "It's a mess, but then again, we've been driving for almost three hours. We might as well find out what's here. Why not try it?"

Why not try it?

I could think of a million reasons why we should not try it, but none of them provided my mind with an escape from our current predicament.

"Sure," we answered with as much feigned enthusiasm as we could muster, and as Ashley gunned it to beat them to the path, I realized that through my fears, I had rarely felt so exhilarated in my life. Here I was, with my best friend by my side, exploring remote lands that few people will ever see.

We descended the side of the mountain to an old rotary at the bottom, and after seeing nothing but overgrown brush in one complete circle, we paused before turning back to our main branch. This time, Bill pulled his Jeep beside ours.

"Let's just go around one more time. There must be a turn we missed," and with that, he drove off in front of us, proceeding three-quarters of the way around again, before turning right onto an even smaller trail, almost completely hidden by the overgrowth. I have no idea how he noticed it.

We followed him.

Tree branches reached out to scrape my dad's car as Ashley carefully maneuvered the wheels onto two warped wooden planks that had been strategically placed over a ditch, and slowed to a stop next to their already parked Jeep, beside a small, decrepit house that Bill and Mark were about to enter.

With rushed glances, we granted each other permission to swallow our trepidation and investigate.

The open door revealed a tiny kitchen to the left, with dirty, broken dishes haphazardly stacked into a bug-infested sink. To the right, red-and-gray checkered vinyl placemats supported three dishes at a small, square table. In the open room ahead, unmade bunks sported rumpled sheets, and blankets stretched toward the bare, uneven floorboards. Two small, broken windows graced the walls on either side of us, and a larger one separated the bunks ahead. A thick layer of black soot obscured the entire scene, preventing even light from entering.

The four of us wandered silently through the remnants of someone's home. Miles from any options, I wondered if they worked at a mine. I wondered what they had mined in this part of the country. I wondered if a family had lived here, if that family had had children. I wondered why they had left one morning, beds unmade, breakfast dishes in the sink, and never returned; if an avalanche had ended it all. I wondered if I alone felt the oddly comforting presence of their spirits.

From the house we followed the men back across the makeshift bridge, halfway around the rotary to another previously unseen spoke, and the road's abrupt terminus at the edge of a ferocious river. The water raced furiously downward, and the scraps of a steel and wooden bridge that once provided its crossing thrashed with the flow in varying states of decay along its shores. On the other side, we watched our path proceed quickly out of the floodplain and zig-zag its way up the south-facing slope of the mountain, into oblivion.

With memories of Zion's Narrows fresh in my mind, I skirted the bank for twenty yards or so, futilely seeking a way to surmount this obstacle, unwilling to allow water to determine the northern and western terminus of our journey for us, even though in truth, it had defined us all along. From the sunset over a Great Lake just one day past the Atlantic Ocean to the deluge in Kentucky that broke us in, from the failed promise of a Texas hot spring to the desert's perpetual thirst, my impressions of our nation revolve around its waters. Sitting on its banks in Zion, the Virgin

River flushed the preconceived notions from my mind of the way life should be, offering for the first time that I should follow no dreams but my own, and then, driving above the crashing waves of the boundless Pacific, I found my future home. Now, a few hours beyond an Alaskan border town with fewer than a hundred residents, the Salmon River precluded our progress and commanded our retreat, once and for all.

Chapter 31
SAVED BY THE JUDGE

(John, 24 years old)

1970: Nha Trang. A coastal resort city on the shore of the South China Sea, with pristine beaches and beachside drinking spots. In 1970, the city had a bustling "entertainment" district centered around the popular Nha Trang Hotel. Just outside the city was Camp McDermott, a major staging area for American troops during the Vietnam War.

It was nearly time for me to return to the states. What could possibly happen?

The day Willie was sent home, I was sent to Nha Trang to be court-martialed for gross insubordination and offering violence to a superior officer.

It had been a few days after we had been told to remain in our bunk area.

I was in the mess hall for midnight chow when I looked up and found two of my least favorite officers suddenly standing at my table.

"Aren't you supposed to be restricted to your barracks?" asked Berner.

"I need to eat."

"Get out of the mess hall now."

After everything that had happened, after losing Jose and others, after being a part of Vietnam for nearly three years, after the heat, the sweat, the mud, the back to back to back sets of bogus orders, after being left on a mountain to be killed, after the Mang Yang Pass, after all of it, with such a short time to the end, this was just too much. I was so close, but something made me put my feet in the saddle and my ass in the sky and it just came out.

"Kiss my ass, sir. Why don't we both get out of the mess hall, you and me? Why don't we go outside, and you take off those bars and we settle this bullshit once and for all? Sound like a good idea to you? Cause it sounds like a great idea to me."

Well, it wasn't such a great idea.

I was court-martialed, but in the end the judge said he felt I had been in Vietnam too long and that there seemed to be, "a lot of people who had too many things to prove."

He fined me the rest of my earned pay for the month, and told them to send me home with an honorable discharge. Then he wished me "Good luck."

I had done it.

With the help of the Almighty and that of a JAG judge who had probably been drafted, I hadn't carried a weapon for a year and a half in Vietnam, I had continued to do what I had been sent there to do, I had paid my debt to my country, I had stayed out of jail, and I had gotten an honorable discharge.

It was February of 1970, I was 24 years old. I was Pvt. E2 Hourihan. I was sitting in a metal folding chair in a huge but nearly empty gray room in the Oakland Army Base, and I was headed home to become civilian John Hourihan again.

I had been out of "the world" too long, and in so many ways I was not the same.

Chapter 32
WHAT IT IS, WHAT IT SHOULD BE

(Mandy, 21 years old)

1998: Drummond, Montana: With a population of a few hundred, Drummond "lies in a mountainous area with the beautiful Flint Creek Valley as one of its many scenic areas. The Garnet Mountains are nearby, and throughout the area you will find abundant wildlife, historic sites known for silver mining since the 1860's and limitless recreational opportunities. One can visit old mining town such as <u>Garnet</u>, set high above Drummond. Recreational opportunities abound and include <u>fly-fishing & ice fishing, big game hunting</u>, snowmobiling and winter sports."

• TownOfDrummondMontana.com

"I'll have the steak," I was the first to place my order at the only diner in the town of Hyder, Alaska. We had returned from the glacier that afternoon and agreed to join our new friends for dinner.

"You don't want the steak," the waitress answered, flatly.

"How about the roast turkey dinner?"

"Nope. Don't want that either."

"Um, what do I want?"

"The halibut."

"Okay, then, I'll have the halibut," I acquiesced.

"Good choice."

"I'll have the halibut, too."

"Me, too."

"Make that four."

After the most delicious fish and chips I have ever eaten, we resisted Bill and Mark's suggestions that we spend another night with them at the local campground, paid our tab in Canadian dollars; the only currency used in Hyder, and parted ways. As we passed through the breezeway, the wall to our left held a large, rectangular bulletin board with two notices tacked to its crumbling cork: a job posting for a waitress in the diner, and an ad for a $400 a month, two-bedroom apartment. I paused long enough to consider both. My high school experience waiting tables at Bergson's Ice Cream and Sandwich Shop would probably fulfill the prerequisites for the job, and even if it didn't pay much, I felt certain it would be enough to cover that rent. In truth I'm not sure that I even liked Hyder much at all, but I was intrigued by its distance, both literal and figurative, from everything I had ever known. Instead, I dutifully retreated to the Jeep when Ashley informed me that she wasn't willing to return my dad's car by herself and explain that she left his daughter in Alaska. That night we stopped in Alberta at four o'clock in the morning to jumpstart a wounded vehicle on the side of the road, and then returned to our nation through Glacier National Park sometime what I think was the following evening. When the customs officer asked us how long we had been out of the country, we groped our tired minds for an answer, and she recommended we pitch our tent there for the night.

We made one more memorable stop before returning east, camping next to a creek on the eastern edges of the Bitterroot National Forest near Philipsburg, Montana, stopping at the Wagon Wheel Cafe in nearby Drummond for breakfast and bottomless coffee, and lastly, on the recommendation of our waitress, at the well-maintained Garnet Ghost Town, which disappointed slightly after having just witnessed the real thing. That night I allowed myself to imagine an alternate universe in which I owned land far beyond the reaches of Missoula, and passed mornings alone in a rustic wooden rocker on the back porch of a house I had built, sipping my coffee, reading the paper, listening to the singing birds and the babbling water, and watching my two large black-and-tan mutts jostle freely through my expansive yard, as they traipsed through a thin row of trees to the ambling creek they buffered, and then returned as gleefully soggy, partners-in-crime. In the distance, snow-capped mountains pierced the infinite blue sky. With a faded flannel over a tee shirt and torn blue jeans, I shifted my baby blue 1980 Chevy Silverado into gear and glided over the dirt road into town. Everyone there waved to me and greeted my dogs who obediently stayed in the back of my truck, unleashed. As a teacher at the local high school, I seemed to know everyone, but really knew no one.

After passing up the lives Hyder and Drummond offered, we traversed the upper Midwest with minimal stops, returned my dad's Jeep to the parking lot of his one-bedroom apartment two months, a thousand bucks each, and over ten thousand miles after borrowing it, and spent another night on the fold-out couches in my mom's living room. My family and my home had disintegrated in my absence and were replaced with an elite liberal arts education, a newfound confidence in my ability to navigate the open road, and a determination not to let it matter.

Chapter 33
HOMECOMING

(John, 24-30 years old)

1970- 1976: Milford: Southwest of Boston, along the Mass Pike and a short skip south on 495 is the factory town of Milford, Massachusetts. It is famous for its pink granite, baseball and its shoe shops. In 1970 it was nearly half Irish and half Italian, the numerous shoe shops had dwindled to one and its granite quarries had closed. Milford was where I had lived as a child, and it was where I returned to after the war, even though I was housed in the next town over, Hopedale.

At the age where most people step out of college and begin their adult life, I was stepping out of one war and right into another. I was headed back to Hopedale, Massachusetts, USA to search for America and its promised dream, and although I figured I had probably earned it, I didn't even know what that dream was.

For the first time in five years I was totally in charge of myself, but it seemed the me in charge was on vacation, or, more accurately, missing in action.

I had left an Asian land filled with explosions, filth, death, heat, chemicals sprayed in the water and in my face, and all the Diet-Rite cola that had been pulled off the shelves in the states because it was poison sent to us to be mixed with Jack Daniels, a place where I had, ironically, become comfortable. Within a blurred day and a half I had landed at

Logan International Airport with all its American cleanliness, safety and fast-food hamburgers. My bone-deep discomfort was surprising, constant and grew with each minute.

Welcome home.

Walking through the crowd of travelers in the polished and chrome expanse of the terminal, I was either ignored, glared at, or in one instance spit at by a teenage girl in a red miniskirt and white peasant blouse carrying a down-filled blue parka and clutching her boyfriend's arm. He at least had the good sense to look worried. There was nothing in the experience of my past handful of years that gave me a clue as to what was happening.

Then, in the parking lot before the hour-long trip back home, when my brother Dennis' request to drive was met with horror from my mother and sister Sheila, their adamant refusal told me there was more to this situation, but I was four years tired. An explanation would have to wait.

After a few days at home, I began to sleep in the daytime, against my mother's complaints that she wanted to talk with me. The avoidance of daytime was not a mental thing. It was physical. The glare from so many shining and waxed automobiles and the reflection of the sun off so much glass in the buildings hurt my eyes. We had been told in Pleiku not to wear sunglasses while in country if we could avoid it. Now I knew why. After the first daytime excursion, I had a headache for days. Every reflection of the sun seared my eyes. Every loud noise or shout dropped me back into the red clay of Pleiku for a mind twisting second. Those miniskirts, which I had never fully experienced before returning, were driving me crazy, and the cement sidewalks hurt my feet.

I woke at dusk, ate and went in search of an EM Club or its equivalent, someplace dark with something to drink. The nights were an endless string of bars, the Co-Mac, The Brass Rail, The Tradesman, The Rod and Gun, the VFW, the Rose Garden, the Blue Moon Saloon, Joe Bats. I enjoyed the similarity the bars had with the safety of the sandbagged enlisted men's clubs. It kept me inside more than out. When I did peek outside the comfort of the smoke, hazy neon lights, and the familiar lineup of bottles behind the bar and their reflection off the mirror, I stood just outside on the stoop and watched the cars on Main Street, an endless string of headlights, tail lights and engine noise, driven by anonymous people who, presumably, didn't want to kill me. What was missing was the omnipresent knowledge that I didn't own the night. There were no illumination flares in the sky, no gunships, no explosions, and no new orders in the morning. I should have been comfortable, but I wasn't. It was winter in New England, below zero, windy, snowy, and I shivered all the time except when I was covered with a quilt or very drunk.

One of those lonely nights, half drunk, on the stoop in front of the Co-Mac bar, and hypnotized by the sight of my own breath in the frigid air, I was approached by an old friend. Wally had returned a year before me. He sat down beside me on the cement step silent as an angel in the fog.

"You have to get out of here," he slurred.

"What?"

"If you don't get out of here you are going to end up like me." I looked at him in confusion.

"Heroin," he said. "After a while it's the only thing that works." He paused, then added, "They hate us, you know." He nodded toward the cars passing by on Main Street in our home town, the town where we both went to school. "We embarrass them."

I didn't pay attention then, but I kept his words in mind.

I drank a lot and smoked more. I altered my consciousness to a point where I could forget the past and block out any possible future. Old friends were afraid of me even though I felt like an empty eggshell, fragile and totally out of any element I was comfortable with. The hate that began to fill me wasn't left over from the war as everyone thought. I had sloughed that off at the club the night before leaving. The anger was because of the latent hatred I had faced since I had returned. This new world was in so many ways more hostile, hateful and deceiving than anything a war can manufacture. It quickly became clear to me that, for the most part, the America I had returned to wouldn't have cared all that much if I had died. I would have become a name to be etched in granite and forgotten except for a few precious moments on Memorial Day.

When friends shared college stories, no one wanted to hear what I had been doing for the past four years. Hippies hated me for things I didn't do. And because I was honest, vets distrusted me for the things I did do, even though I had been awarded the Cross of Gallantry "for valor in the face of the enemy." And when I looked for a job there was no one willing to "take a chance" on a Viet vet like those crazies on TV and in the movies. We vets were pushed beyond what we could accept until we lost our tempers, and then they said, "See, they're crazy." My anger had begun growing from the minute that kid spit at me.

Then, after about a month or so, I rethought what Wally had said. I needed to stabilize. All of us returning needed stability. We didn't get it, and our anger was blamed on a country halfway around the world, washed by the South China Sea, by those whose fault it actually was.

My family had always been a grounding force, but during the three years I spent overseas I wasn't the only one whose situation had changed. And there was no place in the church for a combat vet.

My brother Dennis was a brilliant and promising young guitar player and singer when I left, and who had been working his way up the ladder with a friend who later started a band called Aerosmith. I didn't know what had happened, but when I returned, he was spending most of his time locked in his room listening to Johnny Cash and the Beatles. He later went for help and I went to meet his counselor a few months after

I was home and found out the son-of-a-bitch didn't even speak English. What help could he possibly be?

My oldest sister Pat had been divorced. She had left her idyllic rural home and teaching job in a small elementary school to live in Boston with a school teacher who talked down to me about the politics of the Vietnam war. He admitted confidentially to me that he didn't think "all Viet vets were insane." He knew, he said, that some of them hadn't committed the atrocities being assigned them by John Kerry a new politician who was making a living off a purple heart he reportedly got for shooting himself by accident. Pat was very loving but had her own problems to deal with. Later she married a much better man.

Diane, forced to grow up too soon during our trip to Arizona, had been divorced for the second time, had become born again, and had moved home with her four wonderful kids, Deanna, Joey, John and John. She kept the youngest tied to a tree in our back yard while she sat in a lawn chair in the sun and tried desperately to maintain her sanity. One day when I was up in the afternoon and headed to my car to replenish my beer supply, I cut him loose and told him to "run like hell." She was very upset.

One of the twins, Nancy, who had always defended me when we were kids, was righteously divorced, but she was little help to me because she was busy raising her three boys by herself, working and going to college, and her twin, Sheila, was married and doing fine with three boys of her own, and again, was busy with her own life.

The baby, Neil, was playing baseball for Hopedale High School on the state championship team and in Milford on the American Legion powerhouse. I followed the teams everywhere they went. It kept me sane for three or four hours at a time, three days a week, during baseball season.

Without the burden of feeding kids, except for Diane's, my mother was poised to leave my father who was drinking even more than ever, and again he saw me as a threat to his authority.

The stability I had hoped would welcome me back, the warmth of a grateful country or the stabilizing cement of a loving family didn't exist. Added to that, I was an alcoholic, pot head, anger stuffed, paranoid, twenty something who had just spent too many years in a war and who hung out with a guy who occasionally wore a gorilla costume and climbed the street lights in the center of Milford.

I had lost all respect for rules, the people who abided by them, and the people who made them.

I was like those children in uniform in the Tan Son Nhut airport looking for someone to tell me what I was supposed to do next, and there was no one there.

One night I walked into the Kettle and Keg and met some old high school friends sitting around a table in the center of the room. One was Bilagio and one was the valedictorian I had dated once in college. She was striking with jet black hair and the face of one of those dark-eyed Italian beauties. She had just returned from San Francisco and liked to feature herself as a hippie. We began dating and moved in together in Boston.

I needed to return to civilization, and she needed to piss off her mother who had destroyed her high school relationship with a local guy who had somehow managed to avoid the draft and Vietnam.

We should have listened to God when He had lightning hit a tree near the church and dropped the big oak right across the front door on the day we were supposed to be married. But we ignored the warning of the Almighty and got married the next day anyway. It probably saved my life, but it came at a heavy price.

On our honeymoon she shut me off; partly because she felt she had married down and felt I had to be changed, and partly because she was probably correct. Sex was to be the reward in her behavior modification effort. When we spoke of our honeymoon from then on, the reason we settled on was that I had forgotten my sandals, and we were at a beach resort, and I had to wear boots with my cut-off shorts to town to buy some flip-flops. And that walk "embarrassed" her. Wally was right, I thought.

Over this, we hardly spoke for weeks. It was to be the way of our marriage for twenty-six gut-wrenching years. I was an embarrassment and "inappropriate" to my wife, just as I had been to my country.

Shortly after we got married, I returned to college on the GI Bill. She, and several members of her family, took credit for it.

After a particularly drunken mistake at a family graduation party - where I punched a relative-in-law for suggesting his political pull had been the reason I made it into college, rather than three years of getting shot at in a war zone to earn the money through the GI Bill - I quit drinking, and my life began to clarify.

After the haze that was left from years of long bouts with double-shots, beer chasers and a Jefferson Airplane in the parking lot lifted, I remembered I had always wanted to work at a newspaper and had even had short stint as a reporter in my hometown paper before getting married.

I was determined to return to journalism. The only problem was my wife wanted from me more than what a reporter's position offered, if not in money at least in status, so I took a teaching job at an alternative school in Worcester – fifteen kids who had been tossed from the public schools. I loved the kids and we were making headway, but two years after I had begun, the woman in charge of the school ran off with all the grant money and there was no funding for my position.

Part Four

ADULTHOOD

Chapter 34
WE ALL DIED IN VIETNAM

(John, 30 -48 years old)
1976 - 1995

Mandy was born, and I was chased through the cauterized halls of the hospital by ghosts of Milford wiseguys, angry nuns, the Mang Yang Pass, Saigon hotels, and late night mortar attacks, whores and scores of unpaid willing women, ending in a room with a smiling baby and, "Oh my God, I'm somebody's daddy. What the hell am I going to do now?"

My daughter's birth was the day I was reborn. I don't see how anyone can look into the eyes of a newborn and not see the work of God and the promise of continued evolution.

Vietnam had been a mystical war. No one had survived. We all died in Vietnam. Some of us came back to life, but we came back to life dead. If you can't understand that, you weren't part of that war.

When I saw my daughter in the hospital it was as if something snapped in the universe, as if someone had just changed the channel in my head, and I became a different person. It was what made me sane. I was finally grounded. It is too bad that some of my family and friends never saw the difference and continued to live with what they thought was the old me.

With my newfound stable profession as a teacher and the $1,900 winnings from a lottery ticket, we bought a shit-box house in Uxbridge. It was tiny, but as I explained to my adamantly opposed mother-in-law,

"I know it's small, but if we don't buy something now, we will never be able to get anything. Real estate costs are shooting up, and in a few years we will be able to sell it for a profit and move up."

When my son was born, 14 months after my daughter, we found out that with a family of four and a teacher's salary, we were qualified for food stamps. This was "inappropriate" (a word I would hear a lot from my wife over the next couple of decades) and when Massachusetts voted into law Proposition Two and a Half, and property tax money for schools was severely cut back, I was let go.

"Last in, first out," the superintendent had explained to me. I explained that I might have been teaching four years earlier if I hadn't paid a debt to my country, but he didn't seem to understand what I was talking about.

I was cajoled by my wife to "get a real job."

A childhood friend of hers who was a headhunter surprisingly found a position for me selling envelopes, which was supposedly a real job as opposed to teaching high school. I doubled my pay in one year, and we made money on the Uxbridge house and bought a split level home in upscale Holliston, but it still wasn't enough.

I raised my pay check by taking a job inside at a place where they printed envelopes, then a move to a startup company doing the same work raised it again.

I was moving up financially, but it didn't feel right.

I found I was good at this type of work, and then the wave crashed when I decided to put someone out of business because he wouldn't give us the low price we wanted.

We sold stationery with business logos on it and then bought it from him, marked it up and shipped it directly to the customer.

For a better profit margin, and because the owner of the small printing firm our company used hadn't bent to our price demands, I put his business under.

First I made friends with him, started sending all our business to him until his press time was taken up pretty much totally with our jobs. When his presses were running nothing but our business, we abruptly stopped sending it to him; sent it to a different printing company. His presses were empty, he had no business, he had burned his bridges with other companies, and he could no longer pay his bills.

I found I was pretty good at this "greed is good" thing. I convinced myself that it was what I was supposed to do to work my way up in the financial world.

I had two kids now, and my wife had returned to work. Neither of us liked that the kids had to come home to an empty house.

About a month later the owner called me in.

"John, we need you to spend more time at work."

"I'm giving you 40 hours a week like we agreed."

"Right, and you have raised our profit margin to 30 percent. You'll have to put in just another 20 hours."

"No, I won't do it, not until my kids grow up."

"What do you think I should do with that?"

"You'll get over this idea or you'll fire me I suppose." I walked out of his office and went home to find out the back door had been jimmied by someone just before my kids came home from school, and I called the cops.

A few weeks later my boss opted for the latter. He fired me.

My wife's assessment was, "I can make more money than you can, and obviously you can't keep a job for more than two years."

So we made a decision.

I didn't care who worked. I did care that my kids were coming home to an empty house where someone had tried to break in. I agreed to stay home with the kids. I found out later the kids had jimmied the door themselves.

My mother-in-law thought it funny at Sunday dinner to offer me, "five thousand dollars if you can just keep a job for more than two years." Everyone enjoyed a good laugh at my expense. I didn't defend myself. It had become the way of life. She never paid up.

I loved being with the kids, Mandy woke up and went to sleep with the same smile she kept all day. She was a perfect child. She absorbed the beauty of every day and let it shine from her face, and she ignored anything negative. Mike followed her around like a puppy until they were both in school and became competitive. They both made life a totally enjoyable game that never got dull to play. They brought back the feelings of my Purchase Street home and renewed my family spirit.

But it was an expensive house, so to add to the coffers I decide to go back to work nights, and I took a job part time 9 p.m. to 2 a.m. at a city newspaper as the calendar editor. In the daytime I was still "the Mom." I cooked, cleaned, dressed children, got shots, taxied to summer camps, picked raspberries and made them into jam, put in a new furnace, vacuumed, washed, planned meals, paid bills, took the dog to the vet. The world became a very tired place because that job never ends.

Meaningless people, friends of my wife, looked down on me for some ill conceived belief that I was at home because I couldn't get a full-time job. Without knowing anything, they were willing to believe the worst. I never understood why.

If my marriage had been shaky at best until then, it began here to totally fall apart. My wife had other status markers in mind, and I was convinced to move back to Hopedale, where I had been an Irish punk with a blank diploma and where she had been the valedictorian with a boyfriend who didn't go to Vietnam, and before long that is the history that became our present.

All my life I had wanted to move up, but now I found I was climbing the wrong ladder, and the top had been predetermined to end in Hopedale.

My "friends" were gone, and I now sat in a circle of my wife's friends, most of whom didn't like me all that much, except for the ones who made it obvious they wanted to be as intimate as possible. I didn't oblige them.

When my wife unilaterally bought the house in Hopedale, (My in-laws knew it was to be bought before I did, even took my kids to see the place before I got a chance to.) I took a job at the local newspaper as a special sections editor. Within a few months I was writing the paper's first opinion column.

I guess I wasn't supposed to do that.

"I am going to raise your son to hate you." She actually said it with a vindictive smile. Although I didn't know at the time what it was for, I did recognize that it was retaliation for something.

It wasn't paranoia. She just came right out and said it, standing at the top of the stairs outside his bedroom one night before bed, and then she began to use her degree in psychology and behavior modification to do it.

When my son wouldn't talk to me anymore, I took over coaching his baseball, basketball and soccer teams and he had to talk to me. But there is something strange between an Italian boy and his mother, and even though I coached him all the way through high school - the same high school that had given me a blank diploma - she won.

She raised him to hate me. He bought into it. So be it.

I had come from an inner-city tenement, past the violent poverty of a South Phoenix barrio, through a war, into an upper middle class suburb in a brand new seven-room home with a swimming pool, in a high class development, (which my wife's family liked to call "the projects" when I was around). I had become well known in thirteen towns for my award-winning column and instead of the respect I had earned from everyone else my wife saw it as an embarrassing burden.

When Where You Came From Isn't There

Scrapper Jack had been at a nursing home for months when my sister called to tell me he had been asking for me. I was still upset about how he had treated my family in his younger days, but what harm could it do to visit him?

One morning I drove Mandy and Mike to school, they were in high school now, and I continued on to the nursing home. I walked up the cement walk that cut from the sidewalk straight on through the manicured lawn to the front entrance. I opened the door and realized it was at the door where all appearances of comfort and personal relevance ended. The entryway floor was covered with silt even now in mid-summer when it could easily be swept back out onto the sidewalk. The chairs in the empty reception area looked strangely like the ones that used to be in Biuso's barber shop before Frankie got new ones, red and green vinyl held on with round nut-sized tacks. Some were even cracked at the sides. There were about a dozen chairs lining the walls but only one had the dust wiped away by someone who had sat here for a few waiting moments.

At the window I stood and waited for the teased beehive of hair to turn around from her typewriter. I was waiting for instructions.

"What can I do for you?"

The receptionist was my wife's cousin. I hadn't anticipated that.

"I came to visit my father."

"You need to call ahead," she said and began to turn back toward the half-typed letter.

"He has been asking for me, and I thought …"

"Well, I suppose it won't hurt this one time. Next time be sure you let us know you are coming."

I almost said thank you, but decided against it. I wondered why it could possibly be a rule that family had to call ahead to see someone living here. I had learned not to ask these things, well, not all the time.

I had a rule, respect everyone equally until they show you they don't deserve your respect, then don't respect them. I didn't respect this woman for myriad reasons so I didn't say anything.

She waited for a few seconds. I waited for instructions as to where he might be.

"So, go ahead," she said motioning toward the double doors in front of me.

I pushed the door on the right and it opened into a hallway. I could see a day room ahead of me where old people sat drooping in their wheelchairs, or staring vacuously at the non-functioning fireplace, but he wasn't in there. There were rooms off the sides of the hallway, and I started looking into them all, craning my neck sideways before actually getting to the door. I had the feeling I was doing something wrong, intruding in some way. Then after the third door I realized these people had no expectation of privacy. They turned and looked at me from their rooms as if I were just a fly that had landed on their nightstand.

Then I noticed someone I knew. He had driven me home a few times when I had, at four years old, escaped from kindergarten.

"Do you know where I can find my dad?" I asked.

He pointed from his chair in front of the TV in his room by lifting his right hand and pointing directly over his right shoulder. "Down there, two doors."

I stood in front of my father's door. He too was sitting in a chair facing his TV, but it wasn't on and he was looking out the window.

Scrapper Jack had contracted Parkinson's disease and the medicine they were giving him played a number on his head.

"Hi Dad," I said entering the room.

He nodded and looked back out the window.

"Smiler's up," he said.

Smiler was my mother's brother and one of my father's best friends and longtime teammates in basketball.

"Up where?"

"At the plate." He turned and looked at me with a smile that held a tinge of disgust for me not knowing there was a baseball game going on in the empty field outside his window. Not only that, but it was being played by 80-year-old names from the past.

I sat down on his bed content to "watch" the game.

"Don't sit on the bed. They don't like you to sit on the bed in the daytime."

"Who?"

"Don't sit on it!" he demanded. It sounded as if he was speaking in someone else's voice.

I stood up. "Can we smoke in here?" I asked.

He rose from his game and motioned me to follow him to the hall where there was a line-up of more green vinyl and chrome barbershop-type chairs. The walls and the ceilings were the color of an off-white dinge, and the place even smelled like the old barber shop on East Main.

I looked for an ashtray as he took his place in what must have been his special chair, one chair from the door.

I peered around the corner and, of course, there was a pedestal ashtray, chrome stand and dark amber glass tray.

I picked it up it and returned, set it down between the two chairs and sat down, but as I lit my cigarette, my father reached over and pushed my shoulder. "Get up. You can't sit there."

"Why not?"

"My son Johnny might come in. That's his chair. Say, who the hell are you anyway?"

I took a long drag of my cigarette and stared into his eyes for a very long few seconds. He had no idea who I was. I'm not sure he knew who *he* was.

"No one of consequence, I guess."

"I didn't think so. Get out of that chair."

He stared at the wall across from us, took a long drag on his cigarette and then said, "So who did you come to see?"

"No one."

I got to my feet and said good bye.

"So do you know my son Jocko? He's about your age I think."

"Not really."

I left. I returned only for his funeral.

My eulogy started, "Scrapper Jack was a shoe worker, a fighter and an Irishman, not in that order. He earned a quarter of a million dollars in his lifetime, in the shoe shops of Milford, a nickel at a time."

While I was saying the words, I realized how far my life had come from where my father's had ended, how each generation naturally pushes out past its parents' frontiers. That's the American Dream I guess, to be free to push forward in your own way, in your own direction, toward your own goals, and to reach a point of your own choosing past what your parents could reach, then to leave your children to start on a higher plane with the freedom to do the same.

There was a problem with the American Dream that my father's death pointed out. I had only recently realized I was climbing the wrong ladder and that in order to keep progressing I had to reassess my goals and start over.

I wasn't where I wanted to be. I was climbing someone else's stairway, and the middle class home in Hopedale had been the goal, but not my goal.

There was only one thing holding me back.

Our marriage had run its course. Both sides could be faulted. Then when my son went to college, leaving us alone in the house, it just ended.

Twenty-six years. She told me to be out by August 1 – she gave me a watch as a going away present.

Two months later she asked me to come home.

"Yeah, I ain't doing that anymore."

We all have angels in our lives. In order to make it to his goal, my father had married his angel. Now I had to find mine if I was to make it to where I wanted to be. I wasn't there yet, but at least now I was on the right ladder.

Chapter 35

YOU'RE NOT SUPPOSED TO CROSS THE YELLOW TAPE

(Mandy, 21 - 22 years old)
1998-1999

"Excuse me. Excuse me," with slivered eyes scanning only the ground, I attempted to circumvent the unlikely crowd in front of the yellow caution tape blocking the street which held my office. With a sigh and my gaze firmly down, I continued down Causeway to Canal Street, in an attempt to go around the block and enter Friend Street from the connecting alley.

Last night had been a late one, one which gave me reason to be thankful I had not yet opted for a career in teaching, with its early morning wake-ups. Billy Joel had graced the stage at the Fleet Center, formerly the Boston Garden, only a few hundred yards from where I stood. As soon as the concert was announced, I had charged two tickets on my second new 0%-financing-for-six-months credit card, as my $20,000 salary covered only rent, utilities and the occasional splurge of a grilled cheese sandwich. When I asked Ashley if she would go with me so I wouldn't have to go alone, she was willing, not eager, and suggested it may be a good opportunity for a date with the friend I had been flirting with since we both illegally joined the same summer league team for the end of season tournament. When I proved too weak to ask him directly, my friends stepped in to help. During dinner at a friend's house, I offered the ticket in a blanket invitation to my entire group of friends. Everyone except John knew to have prior commitments, leaving him as the only option. It worked, and although he didn't know it at the time, December 2, 1998 was my first date with my husband.

We started with dinner at my favorite cheap Italian restaurant in the North End, helped with lyrics at Billy's request during "We Didn't Start The Fire" when he explained it would be a train wreck if he forgot the words, and laughed at Mr. Joel's admonition to the crowd of fans' willingness to take relationship advice from an aging three-time divorcee. Then we stopped for a drink, took the green line to the red line back to Davis Square, walked to his apartment together so that he could drive me home, talked about his long-distance girlfriend until I finally took it as a hint, and I walked the last mile across Medford and into Somerville to my apartment, alone.

I had gotten home late and stayed up reviewing the evening with Ashley until almost morning. That morning, when I had stepped onto the #89 bus at the first stop on its route, I swiped my AAA card instead of my monthly bus pass, and the bus driver chuckled while letting me board. He knew me by this point, as I was the first one on his route every morning, and I rode the bus all the way to its terminus at Sullivan Square where I boarded the orange line to North Station. He knew me so well that the night I tried to save money by taking public transportation home from Logan Airport after a late arrival, he drove me all the way to my door, declaring it not safe for me to walk alone, with my luggage, past the projects, in the middle of the night. In my defense, the public housing on North Street in Somerville never seemed so dangerous to me.

When Where You're Going Isn't There

As I turned the corner toward Canal Street on this morning after my only Billy Joel concert, a river flooded my path. Assuming a broken water main was causing the delay, I returned to the end of Friend Street, calmly slipped through the gathered crowd, and stepped gingerly over the caution tape. As soon as I had achieved separation from the crowd, I was stopped by a uniformed firefighter.

"Ma'am," he started with remarkable restraint, "You can't be here."

"I know, I saw the water, but I have to get to work. I work in that building right there," as I lifted my eyes for the first time to meet his and to point to my office, I saw the smoke. He watched my realization and waited for me to continue, and I changed my haggard tone only slightly. "When do you think I'll be able to get into the office? We have papers in there that we have to bring to Minnesota tomorrow for a national conference. I'm supposed to make and ship all the copies today."

"Not today, ma'am. You'll have to step back behind that tape," he turned back to the furniture warehouse building adjacent to mine and its eight alarm fire, and I stood frozen for a moment before joining two of my coworkers standing just a few steps away in the front of the crowd on the other side of the tape. I had only worked there for two months, having secured a permanent job assisting with event coordination during a lunchtime conversation about hosting Ultimate Frisbee tournaments while temping for them. I already felt ownership over their upcoming convention, and I wasn't willing to fly to Minnesota without doing my job.

The three of us regrouped at the bank of payphones in the Fleet Center, on a patch of hallway that had seemed so different than it had previous evening. We called our boss, already in Minneapolis, and I was elected to explain the situation to him, because I was not afraid of his bark, or because he would not bark at me. He listened calmly, told me not to worry about things I could not control, and asked me to put my colleague on the phone. She was only a few years older than I, and bore only slightly more responsibility.

She hung up with direct orders to enter the building at all cost, find the necessary papers, and get the job done.

The third woman, with seniority over both of us, told us she'd take care of it. She had digital copies of all the files we needed, and she'd go to Kinko's and work from there. She told us we didn't get paid enough for this, and to enjoy an unexpected day off. We walked around the city discussing life and potential future relationships and stopped for lunch at a vegetarian restaurant in Chinatown, where she never bothered to mention to me that "beef with broccoli" was in quotation marks for a reason. We and the copies made it to Minnesota on time, the convention was a raving success, and I even had a minute for Christmas shopping in the Mall of America, which was directly across an eight lane highway from my free, fancy hotel room.

Who Says You Can't Go Back?

Before spring began to thaw New England, I took my Frisbee on the road. My return to Mardi Gras, this time by car, was far less eventful than the previous year, and marked the beginning of my longest stretch of Ultimate tournaments; I either played or coached for Swarthmore, every single weekend from Valentine's Day through the Fourth of July. Even in my tight-knit group of Ultimate tossing friends, only John shared the extent of my dedication, and we became travel companions before technically dating. One Friday morning in April, I sat at my desk on Friend Street, realizing I had no plans for the weekend. A quick search revealed a tournament in New Jersey and a women's team looking for more players. I emailed my friend, and asked if she'd go with me. She instantly agreed, but neither of us had a car or the money to rent one, so my next email was to John, who, it turned out, not only had a car, but also plans to go to the tournament with his roommate and a hotel room already booked. We could hitch a ride and crash on their floor, as long as we were at my apartment, ready to go, by 5:00.

We both left work early, and at 9:30 that night, John honked the horn. They assured us we didn't need to worry. John drove fast and this way we'd avoid rush hour traffic. I made the necessary introductions for my friend, and we were on the road, along for the ride.

Three hours later we stopped at a rest stop just outside of New York City because John knew he'd find a giant map on the wall, and it would point him in the direction of the Days Inn, which he knew was on Route 1 somewhere north of Princeton, definitely in the state of New Jersey.

A half hour after that, driving through the fog, we noticed a Days Inn as we passed it, turned around, parked, and learned that they had neither a record of John's reservation nor any rooms available. The Indian hotel staff took pity on us and called around looking for a room with cheerful persistence matched only by the extent of their failure, until they relented and turned to each other with visible skepticism.

"Should I try …?"

"I don't know …?"

"It's the only one …"

"Yes, but …"

We interjected. "We'll take anything! We're not picky. Any place we can sleep for a few hours."

"Alright," the first woman said, cautiously. "I'll call."

She called and secured us a room for $75 per night, $20 more than the Days Inn would have charged, but split four ways, it would be almost affordable for me and was no problem for the others. Then the second man gave us directions.

"Okay," he began, pausing to examine our group. "Who's driving?"

"I am," John stepped forward.

"Okay," he repeated, turning toward John, toward the fog that hung over the parking lot like a blanket, looking uncertain. "It's easy, really. You just go out here and follow this road a little bit until you see 522, and then you follow 522 all the way to the Freehold. It turns left, but you follow it. It turns right, but keep following it. You follow it half an hour, more maybe, until you reach the Freehold. Then you cross 33, and you turn right. Look for The Flame hotel on your right."

"The Flame?"

"Yes, The Flame. It is not so great, but they have a room for you. Tell them we sent you. They will take good care of you. We have a room for you tomorrow night. Our best room, for only the rate you reserved. We are very sorry for the confusion. Good luck."

"Okay," we exchanged nervous thank yous and returned to the car.

We followed country road 522, without a map, for twenty miles, until it ended at a stop sign and T intersection into a route numbered 537 in what we imagined was a sleeping downtown Freehold at what was now 2:30 in the morning. We never crossed any road number 33.

Two months later, John bought his first cell phone, but tonight, none of us had one.

We turned left and stopped at a payphone on the side of the road. John's roommate hopped out to make the call and came back shaking his head.

"Where is it?"

"I don't know," he laughed, incredulously.

"Didn't you call them?"

"Yes."

"Did they answer?"

"Yes. They answered. I told them I was in downtown Freehold and needed to know how to get to their hotel, which is in Freehold. The man from the hotel said 'I do not know. I am not driving.' Then he hung up the phone."

"I guess we just drive until we find it? The town can't be that big."

We turned back and travelled the other way on 537 for only a minute or two before finding Route 33, and guessed that we should go right. After another mile we reached a seven-way intersection with an open gas station, and John parked and went in to ask directions. After a brief conversation, the man started pointing, sequentially, down each and every spoke out of the rotary, and I lost my last ounce of faith and went in to buy a map. Once inside, John could not understand why I wanted a map and assured me that he knew what he was doing.

He chose one of the spokes labeled 33 and drove over the hill, into the three a.m. fog. When we crested the hill, a sign emerged from its top, and we simultaneously exclaimed "WAWAAAA!" and stopped the car one more time.

Unlike three of us in the car, my friend had gone to Williams, far from the Mid-Atlantic, and had never seen such a sight. We shopped quickly for Gatorade and PowerBars and checked with the young man as he mopped the convenience store floor.

"We're looking for The Flame. Is it in this direction?"

"Have y'all BEEN to The Flame before?"

"No, why?"

He chuckled and spoke to his mop. "Yep, it's in this direction."

We paid, and a mile down the road we found our destination. Its lawn ornaments were thrown into an empty pool, and as we parked, a slovenly, middle-aged man wearing only a wife-beater and boxers walked down the sidewalk in front of our car, knocked on the Plexiglas window, and collected for his mail. Our $75 room was yellow from cigarettes, and its smoke detector hung askew a few inches from the ceiling, disconnected. The bathroom door did not shut, and as we pulled out our sleeping bags to lay on top of the disgusting bedding.

"Set the alarm for 6:30," I told my friend.

"I can't," she apologized.

"Why not?"

"There's no clock."

"Oh, okay. Well, call for a wake-up call."

"There's no phone."

When I arrived at the fields the next day, before finding my team, I found some college friends who had come from DC for the tournament and secured floor space for the night just in case. It was unnecessary, though, as John's room did come through at the Days Inn as promised, and as always, John's unplanned adventure worked out in the end.

Chapter 36
IS THERE A MULTIPLE OF DÉJÀ VU?

(John, 48 - 51 years old)
1995 - 1998

My divorced life had begun many years earlier. I just hadn't known it. I was about to find out.

Finding the angel who would help me progress would take some time, but some of the initial steps had already been taken.

First, I needed a place to sleep.

I had spent a week of searching through real estate ads after work and on two weekends, and I was depressed by the time the agent drove up Purchase Street, past Dan's house, past the house of Dorothy Blanche, past Spike's house and then beyond Gonheu's Field where I had played ball as a kid. Things brightened when she took a right just before the house of Linda Chalmers. None of them lived there anymore, but it didn't change the feelings of home.

The hovel at 197 Purchase Street was long gone too, but the bank had sold the property it had foreclosed on to a developer, and here we were parking in the back field where the DeBoer's chicken coops had been.

Shadowbrook was a condominium complex. Before we stepped out of the car in the parking lot I knew I would be living here.

The air in the breeze smelled like the familiar oak and pine forest surrounding us. In the white noise of the woods I could almost hear Woody singing "**The Old Chisholm Trail**."

The crows and the August cicadas sounded like home. It felt as if I would any minute see a pack of kids coming out of the woods near the granite quarry we called "The Hole" armed with Red Ryder BB guns and Davy Crockett hats. I smiled to the agent. She smiled back and said, "Nice woods, huh, and the dumpster is right here in the corner so you won't have to walk far."

At the door to the complex I stopped for a few seconds and looked around, which prompted the woman to sell again. "It's a very safe neighborhood. It used to be a farm I think."

The apartment was a third-floor, three-room walk up. It had an almost Spanish decor of white stucco walls and rounded arches between rooms, with a balcony that overlooked the stand of birches where we had hid from the bad guys or sat and traded baseball cards with Robbie Jenkins. It was surrounded by my woods, the ones my grandmother said were "owned by God," and were therefore safe, and it was a perfect place to start over. I signed a rental agreement and moved in that week.

Having experienced 26 years of long bouts of being married but alone, I was ready to date within a week of the separation being filed. I was 49 years old and, of course, the first person I dated now was a woman I had dated first when we were kids. She had been divorced for a while, and as my attorney said, "Good for you. She is the best looking woman in the county."

She turned out to be a good friend, and although we spent long nights over a few Rolling Rocks and even dinner at my new apartment, we never became intimate – kissed once, but nothing of significance. She advised me to go on with life as if my life hadn't changed all that much and "the right things will happen for you. ... You are the most sensitive person I know. You deserve to find the best. So keep your head, but start looking."

There were others, blind dates with friends of friends who carried emotional grappling hooks and began immediately going places I could tell were down the wrong roads. There were old friends with new ideas, and new friends with old ideas, and as I sat back on the couch after months of sleeping with a woman I didn't much like, I began to think of the advice from my beautiful friend – the best looking woman in the county.

It was becoming obvious that I wasn't going to have a difficult time dating. Everyone was saying yes.

I decided I would take by friend's advice and not settle for anything but the best person I could find.

I began working out in the morning. I ate right, went to work every day just as always, and coached in late afternoons, then during basketball season I did the high school play-by-play for local TV at my alma mater. I stopped chasing people and the advice worked.

A knock at my door one evening while I was watching Monday Night Football over a glass of wine and a pizza, would add excitement and fun to my next few months. She was younger by about fifteen years and was one of those women who could snap men's necks just by walking past them in a crowd wearing tight jeans and a halter top. She was intelligent and lovely. She was exquisite.

We played for several months until she mentioned that she saw me watching a mutual friend at a basketball game and wondered if I had been dating her. "She left home. She's getting a divorce." She wasn't upset, just curious.

I was surprised at the news of this well-known woman leaving home since everyone in town knew her as the "church lady" who taught religion to children as a CCD teacher and studied religion with priests as a master catechist. I had noticed her years ago when she had brought some of her five children to be coached by me in basketball and baseball. She had always been beautiful, but we were both married and our relationship had never gone beyond an occasional glance of recognition. I had also noticed her because she worked at the same newspaper I did. We seldom worked together and even more rarely spoke to each other, but I knew she was a good writer, even as a stringer she was better than most if not all of our salaried reporters. Most of the men in town felt that someone who looked like that and was built like that was a waste as a devoutly religious woman.

I hadn't seen or even thought about her for years, but from then on I began looking around for her.

Her daughter played basketball, and I announced her games, and one evening the woman walked into the gym looking like a better version of Loretta Lynn. She had dark, long flowing hair the body of a 20 year old, and, when she twisted her head and looked toward our side of the room, her teal blue eyes appeared to be lit from behind and shone even in the bright lights of the gymnasium.

I took off my headset and leaned back to my cameraman Artie who was sitting a few rows behind me manning the electronics.

"I think I just stopped looking," I said.

Artie squinted up from his audio equipment to watch her walk in like a confident pony across the gym with all eyes on the church lady who fell from grace, living in an oh-so-judgmental town. Her shoulders were back and her head high and she walked right into the teeth of the stares, smiling occasionally to one person or another right into the ice of their glares.

"Wow," I said after she finished her walk to her seat behind the girls' team bench. "She is one tough woman. That's the one I want," I said.

Artie was a good friend. He smiled and said, "Then you'll get her," and went back to setting up for the game.

I planned, relying on another of my personal rules - Before you do something, know what you are going to do next.

It wasn't until the beginning of baseball season, on the cold March throwing-in-the-parking-lot days, that I thought of a way to get closer.

"Hi, Linda, could you help me out," I said assuredly into the phone. "I have just finished a how-to book about coaching youth baseball, and I need it edited. Do you think you could do it? I have a swimming pool."

I couldn't believe I had said the last part, but it worked. I guess she wanted to swim, but she never did edit the book.

Before we could go out in public together I knew, just because of who she was, that I would have to end any relationships with other women. There were only a few at the time, and, although I quickly had figured out how to get people to go out with me, I did a very poor job of "breaking up."

One laughed at my awkwardness and said affectionately, "She's a really good person. I'm happy for you … If you screw it up give me a call." We left as friends.

The other promised to dance on my grave and slammed the door.

I was free to date the church lady.

At first we went out of town. She liked country music and line dancing so we went. She danced and I nursed a beer and watched.

When we walked through the town holding hands a few weeks later, people pulled their cars off to the side of the road and stopped to look in shock.

My baseball players had a field day with my new-found life.

One afternoon in the last inning of a game, I was in the third base coach's box directing traffic when, between batters, a kid who had been my shortstop since he was nine years old, and was now 14 and more of a friend than a player, was suddenly standing beside me sporting a wide smirk.

"What," I asked.

"You better not leave the field, coach," he said smiling.

He looked across to the opposite side of the chain link backstop where stood my ex wife. He looked to her left, where stood the grave dancer, and then next to the dugout was my friend of six months or so, and then Linda the woman I was currently dating.

"I see what you mean."

Our relationship did not go unnoticed.

My players were mostly congratulatory. The older ones were downright envious.

Mandy, my daughter, took it all in stride, "She's cute," she said after meeting her. "She's good for you. You look great." Then she made me promise not to date anyone who was too young to remember black-and-white TV. I immediately bought a black and white TV, just in case.

Of course everything couldn't go all that smoothly forever. At Mandy's college graduation my ex and my current had a day-breaking argument over the words, "Hey Linda, why don't you take this camera and get a picture. You know, just of our family?"

I was standing on a lawn at Swarthmore College, in the sunshine, between two women, one who had a plan and one who didn't want to be a part of the plan. Lin sheepishly took the camera and walked several paces from the group, but when she turned to take the picture I saw she was crying. She stomped her foot and dropped the camera to the ground. One heel of her stiletto shoes broke off and she hobbled a few steps away from us, then took of the other shoe and almost ran up the walkway. I excused myself and caught up to her. She was searching for a cab. She had it in her mind to take a taxi from Swarthmore, Pennsylvania to Hopedale.

The lies we had been facing since we had started dating had taken their toll on Lin and me, and our nerves were raw.

Lin was so devastated that she had hurt my daughter that she was sitting on a bench just off campus, crying almost uncontrollably, and apologizing between outbursts. The clumsy and mean-spirited attempt to hurt the feelings of a good woman and split us up had backfired; instead I fell deeper in love with her.

As for Mandy, a few weeks later she borrowed my new Cherokee and drove off with a friend to tour the United States. She visited the entire country except Hawai'i, she even drove up to Alaska. When she returned she seemed happy enough with our situation.

My son Mike took a side in the whole thing. Not mine. Good for him. He was true to his mother.

Lin's kids were in various stages of shock.

One of her English/French sons, who I had coached as a youngster, visited us in Milford, told jokes about the Irish, asked me not to smoke in my own home, and told me I wouldn't be able to understand what he was studying in college so we shouldn't try to talk too much. I liked him.

One daughter, the basketball player, brought a kid I considered a product of the teenage wasteland to my home and told me it was her boyfriend. It wasn't. I threw his ass out. She apologized. I liked her too.

One, the second son, didn't care about me as long as his mother was happy. He was 15, loved his mother and was enjoying life. I liked him the best.

The youngest girl threw rocks at my car as I drove past her house. She was 10. It was her right.

The rest of the world, except for a few wonderful friends I had coached with, continued to tell fabulous and fictitious stories about both of us. At some point we got used to it.

Lin introduced me to some things quite new that brought back old memories. She enjoyed line dancing to country music, and I remembered I was brought up on Hank Snow (my mother's favorite) and Hank Williams (my father's second favorite, just behind Woody). And she respected me for who I was, not what she wanted me to turn into.

She was also a very religious woman, and although I can't say she introduced me to God, she did remind me that I knew Him from way back.

Then it happened.

"I'd like you to meet my mother and father," she said one afternoon sitting on our balcony.

That night we went. As we stepped out of the car and headed up the steep set of stairs I asked, "How long have you lived in this house?"

"All my life until I got married."

"Do you have a friend named Spooky?"

"She was my best friend throughout my childhood." She looked at me with a dubious squint.

Not too many people have a friend named Spooky, and Spooky was the name of the friend of the girl whose eyes had hypnotized me years ago when I had gone swimming across the street in the lake and was torn away by Mike and Peter because they realized she was "12 years old."

Inside the house, which looked somewhat like a clone of my Purchase Street home, I met her mother and stepfather, Louise and Ken. Ken, I was told, had been called "Reb" since he had moved up here from Mississippi to work on the pipeline. Although neither of us said it, we both knew it was he who had bought beer for me when I was 18 and the drinking age was 21.

"Ever been to Carol's Hamburg Stand in Woonsocket?" I asked.

"Yup." He smiled and nodded, and it was over.

Then Lin, Louise and I sat down on the couch and, almost by rule of law, we started looking at old photo albums.

I got stuck on the picture of Linda at 15 in her bright yellow bikini. "I bought her that," said Louise proud of her daughter, and well she should have been. The girl in the picture was stunning.

On our way home I admitted to her that I had been the guy in the blue suit who stopped and tried to pick her up while she was wearing that bikini and walking down the street to the lake.

Until that moment I had never made a connection, past to present, on these isolated incidents.

We later found out we had also lived a block from each other in Uxbridge, we had both decided to move to Holliston at the same time (then she changed her mind), that she had dressed as sexy as a 14-year-old could so she might impress the young hippie who worked at the gas station near her home from the back seat of her parents' car (me, just after the Army), and my longtime nightmares of an animal pen on a farm on a back road in Mendon where I was frightened by a "monster" that lurked just below the hill in a fenced in area, actually was spawned at a clambake my father had taken me to at Linda's uncle's home when I was 10, and the monster was a pig that attacked children. She was there but she was a baby. All this answered the question I had had for so many years in Hopedale. Why was it that every time I saw this woman I wondered if she was OK. I never acted on this, nor did I go any further than to wonder how life was treating her. And it answered the question why in her junior high school days she had been known by her peers to have an unexplainable serious interest in the Vietnam War.

I have always believed that time bends, and you end up seeing or feeling things in the present from your past or future. These coincidences did nothing to contradict that.

Our connection had been dictated long before we recognized it.

We were married six months after the day I met her parents. I had found my angel. Her kids and mine all came to the wedding, smiled and danced and congratulated us. We were both very thankful for that. There were no more sticks and stones until after the wedding.

Chapter 37
WHAT LANGUAGE WAS THAT?

(Mandy, 22 - 23 years old)
1999-2000

As the first anniversary of my college graduation approached I was living in a city with my best friend, working at an education non-profit, playing so much Ultimate Frisbee that my club teammates elected me captain for the next season. My life was unfolding just as I had planned.

I sat alone in my office, just after five o'clock on a Friday evening when the phone rang. I never stayed this late, but I had an eight o'clock flight, and it didn't make sense to go home first. These were the days when we only had to arrive at the airport an hour before a flight. I answered the phone, and the woman on the other end asked for me.

No one called here for me. My job had disintegrated over the past few months until I was so bored by my responsibilities that I wrote up an entire report for my boss proving that he would save money by returning his copy machine and sending all his jobs to Kinko's rather than paying me do all the copying. In response, my boss took me to workshops with him and engaged me in meaningful conversations regarding them. He appreciated my interests, knowledge, and ideas, but my lack of real experience rendered me useless to him as a trainer.

"Look," he told me on the drive back from a School-to-Work conference in Rhode Island. "I know you're bored here, but I don't know how to use your skills. I'd love to have you facilitate, but no one would listen to you since you don't have any practical experience," he explained, bluntly.

"I can make them listen," I tried to exude confidence.

"It won't work."

"Why not?"

"Because they'd be right."

I have had the privilege of working for several exceptional leaders and enough others to make me realize good fortune when I have had it. The person who can convey respect while pushing me in the direction of growth is the person I want to work for. Even at the time I appreciated his directness and his advice, and although I admired the people and the organization's work, I started looking for other jobs.

Accidental Employment

"Speaking," I said, confused.

After identifying herself by name and company, the woman on the other end of the line explained that she was calling to offer me a job. I had interviewed for a position at a software company in Cambridge on a whim. My friend worked there and enjoyed her job. She said her boss and co-workers were great, it paid better than my non-profit, she wasn't bored at work, and she insisted that they wouldn't mind that I didn't know the first thing about programming. It turned out she was right on all counts.

"Great! Thanks!" I replied, and just before I hung up the phone I thought to ask a very important question. "Could you tell me what exactly the position entails?"

"Of course," as my new supervisor patiently explained my job, I watched the clock scroll past the time I had planned to leave to catch the T, furiously scribbled the details onto a sticky note, thanked her, hung up the phone, and ran out of the office for the airport, without looking back.

By midnight I had arrived in Columbus and found the friends with whom I had planned to share a rental car: a college friend, who had already arrived from DC, and John and Hillel, who had taken a different flight from Boston. Hillel had just moved to Boston from DC less than a week before this tournament. Although I had already signed a lease to move into a house with him and a few other friends later that summer after Ashley left for medical school.

Hillel and I had met for the first time that Monday evening on the Ultimate field. I was at the top of my game, teeming with confidence. The other team didn't have enough players, so we mixed up the teams and played pick-up. Somehow the numbers of women were still uneven, and I offered to cover the guy I didn't recognize who I assumed was on the other team. On the first point, John hucked it to him in the end zone, and I was thankful for the opportunity to prove myself, especially while John was watching. I sprinted for it full speed, confident I had him beat, but when I went up for the defensive block, the disc was already in his hand.

"Try that again," I trash talked, undeterred.

"Sure thing," he confidently retorted.

Over the next few points I learned, quite simply, that he would beat me on every turn, and eventually I stopped offering to cover him, without admitting why.

After the game, when my team walked toward our cars to head to the local bar, he was following us. I stared inquisitively, apparently long enough for him to notice.

"Hi, Mandy," he said with a friendly smirk. "I'm Hillel. It's nice to meet you."

I stopped and looked toward my friends, enraged at them for allowing me to mock my future roommate, but they just laughed, as did he. They kept walking, but he waited for me to catch up, and we began a long exchange of stories of broken noses and sprained knees. We arrived at the bar as old friends, and by the time my food arrived, both he and John were stealing fries off my plate.

That night we piled into the rental car for the hour and a half drive from Columbus to Versailles (pronounced ver-sales), where we would pitch our tents for a weekend of Ultimate amidst their annual "Poultry Days" festival, boasting the best chicken in the world and the crowning of Miss Chick. At a break in the travel conversation, I interjected with my news.

"I think I got a new job today," I started.

"You think?"

"Well, I'm pretty sure. We decided I'd start in four weeks so that I can give notice and still take a road trip before starting."

"What's the job?"

A logical next question.

"I'm not sure, hang on." I loosened my seatbelt to fish the sticky note out of my jeans pocket. It was crumpled and stuck to itself. I flattened it out and started reading it to the car.

"The title is Applications Developer. It's for a company that makes fundraising software for nonprofits. I'll be working with Oracle databases."

"You're going to be programming?" John asked. He was a software engineer, and he knew I was not.

"I guess."

"What language?"

"English?"

"No, what software language?"

"I don't know."

John was driving, keeping a straight face throughout. Hillel, however, was laughing from the passenger seat in front of me. He looked back over his shoulder at me.

"Here," he instructed. "Give that thing to me. There's more light up here."

I handed it forward and laughter ensued.

"What language?" John asked him. I was no longer integral to the discussion.

"SQL and PL/SQL," he answered John, and then he turned to me, shaking his head as he handed the paper back to me.

"What?" I asked.

"It's not spelled s-e-q-u-e-l. It's an acronym. Stands for Structured Query Language."

"Oh," I laughed, too. "Maybe I shouldn't let my boss see this sticky note."

The next morning, my friend and I ditched the women's team to play with John and Hillel's Haverford alumni team. A few hours later, we were chased from the fields by a massive mid-western thunderstorm that washed away our plans. John drove us back to the flooded field when we all wanted to go find food instead, braved the downpour to salvage our tent and belongings from the flooded field, hung them strategically so they would dry when the storm ended, pulled from his bag enough warm clothes for all of us, and drove us to a nearby Kroger's to buy dry blankets before returning for the best chicken dinner I have ever tasted. Everyone else complained of their soggy tents and clothing that night, but we were comfortable and dry. While I meticulously consider every plausible outcome and impeccably plan for all of them, John doesn't need to bother. Just as he had in our New Jersey tournament, and as he would repeatedly in the years to come, he confidently and deftly handles whatever is thrown in his direction.

When we arrived at the airport Sunday night, Hillel asked me how long I had been dating "boyscout." We hadn't been dating that weekend. That came a few weeks later. By the end of that summer, my second post-college life had begun.

I moved from the outskirts of Davis Square, an hour commute to my job that paid next to nothing, to the center of Inman Square, a ten-minute walk to my software job with a real salary and work that felt like solving puzzles. We had saved money by renting a U-Haul overnight to move in, and we were delayed by a lack of packing, a broken foot, a broken thumb, a torn ACL, one-way streets, and several unhelpful tree branches. John and I retreated to his unpacked apartment when we finally finished around four o'clock in the morning, and I returned home by eight to change and walk to work. When I tiptoed into the front door to avoid waking anyone, I found that unnecessary, as only Hillel was home, sitting in the living room, surrounded by boxes, finishing the *New York Times* crossword puzzle.

"Want to go get some breakfast?"

"I'd love to, but I have to go to work. Don't you have to be on campus?"

"Not today. You should call into work so we can go check out the diner across the street."

"Really, I should go to work."

"I've heard the S&S is really good," he said, enticingly, looking back toward the puzzle.

I hesitated only for a second before picking up the phone and calling my boss.

"Hello, this is Mandy."

"Hi, Mandy."

"I'm not going to make it in today. I'm, um, not feeling well."

"No problem. Take the day off. I'll see you tomorrow."

"Thank you."

"You're welcome," she paused before hanging up. "Mandy?"

"Yeah?"

"I didn't expect to see you today. Moving is always stressful. Don't worry about it, but next time you don't have to pretend."

"Thanks," I said, only a little sheepishly.

That morning, Hillel and I walked over to the S&S for the first time. He, I and John returned frequently that year, at all times of the day and night. I'm not sure whether it was their surly wait staff or mediocre food that hooked us.

Chapter 38
GOODBYE AGAIN TO HOME

(John, 53 - 55 years old)
1999-2000

"I'm sorry John," Francis Gubinski, the managing editor, said as he snooped uninvited over my shoulder while I edited a feature story by Carrie, the southern area reporter, "but you can't say Indian. It has to say Native American. You'll have to change that."

There were 11 metal-sided grey desks in the newsroom of the 16,000-circulation Milford Daily News, partitioned off by nothing. It was sort of the open-living concept. There were posters on the wall; a map of the United States, a map of a 13-town area in southeastern Massachusetts, and a yellowed list of state politicians from somewhere in the 1950s. Half of the desks were empty, showing that we had been downsized. There was an ashtray and a dirty coffee mug on each desk.

The editor, Nick, was grumpy and bitter having run this newspaper at times when he had no one who he could call a real reporter, no real editors and sometimes with only one prima donna photographer to cover both news and sports, and who thought her work was "art."

He relied heavily on the wire services, stole from other newspapers, made up stories, ran stories from decades earlier, and pretty much did whatever it took to put out a daily newspaper. It was said he never went out at night because so many people in Milford hated him for stories he had printed in the paper.

They deserved the stories. He didn't deserve the hate. He and Francis had been newspapermen back when newspapers told the truth, and the truth was what caused the anger.

I wasn't really a copy editor, but this was a small paper that had been one of the last in the state to roll over to offset printing, and Peter, who was third in charge, had a BA in English, solid ethics and a good handle on the newspaper business, had asked me to help him out today, so I was editing a story for a reporter so we could get it into today's paper.

Carrie was a sweet, intelligent and attractive brunette with too thick glasses. She was unique in the newspaper business since smart kids coming out of college didn't usually opt for journalism as a career. It was a dying profession, mainly because short sighted people in charge of papers had put their entire editorial content online … for free. The smart grads knew it was nearly over, but it had been her lifelong dream so here she was. She had been standing over my other shoulder and reading along with me, but now she pulled her glasses down so she could look directly into my eyes over the rims.

Francis had started at the paper 37 years earlier and had worked his way up to being the second oldest person in the newsroom, and with his age and longevity at the paper he had become the second in charge, just below his lifelong friend, Nick the editor.

"Fran, it's a feature story about a new Indian restaurant." I tried to explain.

"Yes, but now we have to say Native American." He nodded his head in satisfaction with himself. I swiveled my head and returned Carrie's mouth-open stare.

"What do you think?"

"It's OK with me if it's OK with you," she smiled. "Just take my name off it."

"Native American it is." I hit the button to send the story to the printer. From print, it would be cut to size, waxed and pasted up on the page, and the new owners of Milford's first Indian restaurant would become known for their Native American food. They wouldn't be happy about it.

While I was trying to solidify my position on the paper, Lin's ex had decided to take her back to court to get child support from us. I thought it a bit much since we had, only a handful of months prior, cut his alimony payments from about $800 a month to zero by getting married. We could have just lived together and continued to collect, but it seemed wrong.

In court it was decided that two children would stay with their father and two would come to live with us. Lin was elated, and I was in love, and to me "family" had always meant the same as "self."

Since my Shadowbrook condominium wasn't big enough for four people, we sold it. At dusk the night before leaving, I stood amidst the birches, I peered through the woods at the red brick chimney atop the house that had been the DeBoer's farm house, and, very reluctantly, I said goodbye again to my beloved Purchase Street home, my childhood woods, the crows, the river, the lake I skated on as a kid, and the neighborhood I knew so well.

We bought a half duplex back in Hopedale.

It had to be Hopedale so the kids would be allowed to stay in their beloved high school.

Although I was pretty sure the exorcism had been successful, it seemed the devil kept dragging me back to hell, which for me was synonymous with Hopedale.

Since the oldest of Lin's girls was married and the next two kids in line chronologically were in college, her ex was told to pay us a minimal child support payment for each of the two living with us. About fifty bucks a month was supposed to make everything even.

Because our mortgage had doubled, we were paying more for each utility, and we were now feeding four instead of two, paying for teen clothes, school costs, and allowances, Lin began selling Mary Kay, and I had become Special Sections Editor, opinion columnist and investigative reporter and was trying to make myself as indispensable as I could. I was ready once again to move up the ladder.

While dealing with the problems of teen children again, I managed to also do something positive about many of the problems of my hometown and the towns around it in a way in which no one had been accustomed, since it was the first time anyone was allowed to seriously investigate the goings on of politics and law enforcement.

Suspected corruption in an area police department was one of our first investigations, and at the end of it I got to say goodbye to a cop who selectmen decided had spent money he shouldn't have, had "embellished" on his resume, had beaten some young people he shouldn't have, and had threatened me with retribution for finding out the truth.

"You do what you do, and I'll do what I do, and let's see who is standing in the end," I told him outside the local courthouse when he had threatened me in front of another reporter and several teens who were there paying fines for DUI and disorderly conduct from the previous weekend, and my voice-activated tape recorder which I had left on by mistake.

He stormed off, and about a month later he was fired.

It was fun. I was getting paid to do what I was born to do, telling truth to power.

On the home front, I also got to deal with the sex, drugs and rock and roll of our new yolk of teen children. They were no worse than any other Hopedale teens, better than most, but this situation still hadn't been in the plan.

The only story my publisher wouldn't allow me to print was on the whereabouts of the asbestos from the torn-down Catholic Church, ("I think we'll give God a break, John.") and that night my new step-daughter asked me to have a talk about sex. She was now 13. The most satisfying thing I found out was that she wasn't pregnant, and I found out after a marathon conversation with her sitting on the kitchen floor with my back against the stove, that there wasn't even the possibility that she could be pregnant unless there was some new way for it to happen.

Then we had a talk about drugs.

"Young lady," I told her after both talks, "You are just going to have to deal with the fact that you are a good girl, and you are going to have to live with it."

A few nights later, while standing on the roof of my truck in the dark, I took pictures of a dump that had been ordered closed. It was being used as a transfer station. Someone was probably making illegal money.

My step son needed some kind of focus in his life other than video games, so we bought him a guitar. Turned out he was a natural, and a really good kid to boot. He even began to come in at his curfew.

I wrote about a scam in which some politicians and police were supposedly offered jobs as part of the security team for an arms-selling operation. Several of them it seems had signed contracts even though there really was no operation at all. The whole thing was made up. All the signees had put up money to fund the bogus operation and a young local con man left the area with the cash.

Our paper shamed one of our towns into repaving Main Street, explained the deforestation of a wooded park, helped spur the creation of a Vietnam Memorial, exposed runoff of chemicals from pristine lawns into the lake in the center of another town (The lawn-enhancing chemicals were now feeding the weeds that would eventually choke the man-made pond out of being usable), shed light on PCBs leaking from some abandoned generators into a stream in town, took pictures inside the now closed Draper Corporation showing that all the fire doors had been opened and there were barrels of paint and oil-soaked rubbish in 55-gallon drums, and I got to interview several local and state politicians including Ted Kennedy.

"Senator Kennedy, those of us who have been affected by Agent Orange would like to know how the government in general and you in particular are going to handle the troops coming home from Iraq with strange health conditions."

I don't remember his answer, but I remembered it satisfied me.

Then I asked him, "You talk about the greening of our state and how we have to cut down on our use of fossil fuels." I waited for him to nod. "So I was wondering why your limo is outside running to keep it air conditioned for you, so it will be cool when you leave here?"

He didn't like that question. Didn't answer it.

On the home front, Lin and I dealt with the problems of divorce and children and exes in a town where so many people never vetted rumors

The "stories" being told about Lin and myself by friends and relatives of both our exes, made life a constant adventure of always wondering what we had supposedly done yesterday.

It wasn't long before I lost the coaching jobs that I had held for several years, and one of the reasons given, among several equally untrue reasons, was that I had "contracted a blood disease and was in the hospital." This lie was actually told to some of my players. Some parents called to ask about it.

This never happened. I wasn't sick. I wasn't in the hospital. I had no blood disease, but I did live in Hopedale, a very strange town indeed.

The group of people and organizations that owned the Milford News saw the internet as the end of printed newspaper cash cows and sold the paper to a conglomerate that also bought our direct competition and put the larger newspaper in charge of us.

Then, just before Christmas, 1999, it seemed that everyone at the Milford News who made any appreciable money at all was called in one and fired. It made the paper look much leaner and easier to sell. Which happened.

There were nine months of no job, but even though the baseline child support didn't do much to put food on the table the kids still ate. And the antics continued, with one of our teen girl's new friends threatening to use his new steel tipped boots on me. That didn't work out well for him.

Then, the month that my savings would run out, and I wouldn't be able to pay the mortgage, I got a job interview. The owners of the Conway Daily Sun, in New Hampshire, wanted to start a new newspaper in Laconia. It was to be a daily newspaper and it was to be in direct competition with an entrenched daily a block down the street.

The kids didn't want to move to Laconia. They wanted to stay in their hometown, so they moved back in with daddy, and we started paying child support again. Within a short time for one reason or another both kids told me they weren't living with him. We paid it until the youngest turned 18, and it was all finally over.

We thought.

Chapter 39

LEARNING NEW FLAGS

(Mandy, 23 - 25 years old)
2000-2002

On an unseasonably warm winter walk through Cambridge, John and I shared travel stories. His family adventures crossed an ocean and spanned his entire youth. Mine had been self-directed and crammed into the past couple of years. Those stories quickly revealed our shared desire for exploration, and by the time we reached his apartment we had decided to cross the country together that summer. I didn't have enough vacation time, but my company was so reasonable I assumed I'd be able to take a leave without pay, and if I couldn't, I would quit and find a new job when I returned. John never bothered to consider plans.

Planning proved unnecessary when a few friends who were starting a software company in Washington, DC asked me and John if we'd be interested in moving down there over the summer to work with them. We agreed fairly quickly, moving south from Cambridge by way of a friend's wedding in Ouray, Colorado, a 16-mile trek down the Virgin River in Zion National Park's Narrows, visits with friends and family in Sacramento, Berkeley, Ashland, and Seattle, and a return stop at the Wagon Wheel diner in Drummond, Montana. We arrived in DC in the middle of a massive, late afternoon thunderstorm that had ominously followed us east for hours.

Old friends were plentiful in DC, which was one of the reasons we had chosen to relocate, and they graciously welcomed us into their world.

Life there was set up for us before we even stepped into it. We had a job working together, with friends. They told us which Ultimate teams to play on and when and where the try-outs would be held. I would find a house with Ultimate players, and others already had an apartment lined up with a room for John. In the meantime, we would stay with our start-up co-conspirators and other Frisbee tossing friends in their mainly vegan, except those on the Atkins diet, communal home in a rundown neighborhood's former drug house that has welcomed several dozen of my friends over the last two decades. It was especially convenient for us, as its attic housed our office, as well. Our social calendars were filled with happy-hours and house parties, Ethiopian restaurants and the Common Share, and plenty of Ultimate Frisbee.

Our start-up eventually subletted office space in Dupont Circle, and then moved to a second location down the road, and my own programming skills expanded to an alphabet soup of C++, XML/XSL, Java, MySQL, SQL, PL/SQL. It was not a future I had ever envisioned for myself, but I found the job interesting. I was the only woman in the company, and I struggled to get my ideas heard, even though I felt confident that my friends did respect me. Regardless, I thoroughly enjoyed coming to work each morning to work toward a common goal with my friends.

One morning my friends and I had arrived early and were discussing Ed McCaffery's gruesome broken leg from previous night's Monday Night Football game. We tried to pull up the video to show someone who had fallen asleep early, but the computer wouldn't work. We tried another laptop, and then a third, before realizing that ESPN.com must be broken.

The clock had just passed nine when another friend whose non-profit shared office space with us arrived and found us huddled around a single laptop.

"Are you guys looking up the helicopter?" she asked, fairly casually.

"We're trying to get on ESPN to see if we can find footage from last night's game. What helicopter?"

"I'm not sure. There was a weird news report on the radio as I parked the car. Something about a helicopter hitting a building. It seemed like it might be a big deal."

"A helicopter hit a building? Where?"

"New York, I think. I didn't catch much, and they didn't seem to know much."

Our video attempts had failed, and our search for "helicopter building New York" similarly hung the web browser. The bunch of software engineers retreated to our own laptops, attempting to access several different news sites, while the member of our group whose focus revolved around charity, not computers, switched on the old television.

"Guys, it's on TV," she called us while adjusting the coat hangers rigged to serve as a makeshift antenna.

It had only been half a dozen years since my brilliant next door neighbor had come into my dorm room to introduce me to a brand new application called Netscape, and the concept of getting news from the television had already been eradicated from my mind.

We joined her, and she stabilized the picture in time for us to watch the Pentagon shake behind an unknowing reporter, who had been tasked with discussing events from New York. In stunned silence, we watched live images from New York show the crippled towers crumbling to the ground, we witnessed the reporter's realization that the Pentagon had been struck behind her, we listened to the anchormen theorizing that a fourth plane was headed for the White House, and an eerie calm filled the room as we registered that if that were true, we were likely sitting in its path.

I had chosen to work with my friends because it sounded like fun at the time, but all at once I realized how fortunate I was to be surrounded by people I loved, every day of my life.

We accepted the offered ride home for the camaraderie, although we could have walked the three miles in less time. The next day John and I loaded Joey, the lovable and lazy mutt we had adopted from the local humane society, into our Echo, and drove to John's parents' Houston home. Along the way, American flags adorned every hillside, highway sign, and overpass from Virginia to Louisiana in an outpouring of American patriotism that has not been rivaled in my lifetime. Then we crossed into Texas.

"What kind of flag is that?" I asked John.

"That's a Texas flag," he answered with a wry smile.

I shook my head and braced myself for my introduction to my fiancé's childhood home, which I would eventually come to love.

Chapter 40

THE DEVIL COMES TO PARADISE

(John, 55 - 57 years old)
2000 - 2002

At a mid-winter job interview with the two young rich boys I would later call the Pros from Dover, not in a complementary way, we made the best impression we could in the hopes of building a daily newspaper in Laconia.

During the interview, I couldn't help but notice that the owner, who would ultimately be doing the hiring, didn't seem to care about my credentials all that much, and I wasn't convinced this would be a good place for us.

I should have walked out, but we were out of money and needed the job so I put it on hold.

We drove six hours at a sliding 30 mph in a driving nor'easter, down I-93, back to Hopedale. We arrived tired from the road but determined to get back to New Hampshire as soon as possible so we could lay groundwork for the new enterprise. No one had successfully started a daily newspaper from the floor up for about a century, but we had both been through enough so we just weren't worried about its success. Ads would be the biggest stumbling block, but Lin was my ace in the hole. I figured a woman who had potty trained 11 kids (five of her own and six foster kids) would have the patience and tenacity to sell anything to anyone.

A few weeks later we got the word that we had indeed been hired, and the paper would begin in the spring. We said goodbye to the kids, donated most of our belongings to the Salvation Army, and headed to the lakes region of New Hampshire.

With the money from the sale of the Hopedale house we quickly had enough to move north and stay in studio apartment that no one believed we were going to live in for three months. It was three strides from one side to the other and seven strides the other way. But it had a small fridge and a microwave, a shower and a bed, and Lin and I had already found we had one important thing in common. We loved being with each other.

We snuggled in, got free DVD movies from the library, cooked in a microwave, found Gunstock Mountain and Red Hill, read books out loud, found an inexpensive coffee shop, stayed in bed for days, and began our wait for spring and the time when the paper would begin paying me.

During this time of exploration we found out that the richest people in town were the ones who owned parking lots they could rent out to concession stands during Bike Week and that there was a two party system here; you were considered to be either a Republican or a communist.

We found that in this place, where no one paid state income taxes, the financial void was filled with the sale of cheap booze, which drew people from all the states around because there was no tax at the state liquor store. In one of my first columns I suggested changing the state motto to, "Welcome to New Hampshire. Would you womens like some liquor?" It didn't go over big, but at least everyone was talking about the new free newspaper.

Sitting alone in a plush antique Morgan chair in a coffee shop in the center of Laconia while Lin sold ads for a newspaper that didn't exist yet, enjoying the live fireplace and watching the snow cover the cars outside the window and looking across the street to the Bahamas poster in the window of a travel agency, I prematurely thought how innocent rural New England was – how clean and simple.

On my second cup, I struck up a conversation with what I thought was a typical down-home northern New Englander in big green rubber boots, jean overalls and a flannel shirt and a baseball hat that advertised the local high school teams, "The Sachems."

"D'ya ski?" he asked, not even looking up from his newspaper – our competition.

"Nope, not for a lot of years."

"D'ya drink?"

"Not anymore. I gave it up."

He put his newspaper down, looked at me, tilted his head and asked, "Then what the fuck are you doing here?"

It snowed every day, 3, 4, 6 inches and no one mentioned it. It just happened. It was plowed and everyone went to work and school just as if it were summer and this was rain.

Other than ski, drink and fish there really didn't seem to be anything else to do in the town where they had an annual dog sled race down the main street, and ran the only Indian out of town when he answered a question about the school mascot. He hadn't called for an end to the mascot or anything. He just pointed out that the guy dressed as a Plains Indian, calling himself a Sachem, running up and down the sidelines of football games waving a tomahawk was sort of like the pope running up and down the sidelines of a Catholic school game waving a cross and shouting "Kill the infidels."

The winter deep freeze melted into what passed for spring in Laconia, and on the first day of work Ed Westwood, the publisher from South

Dakota who had invested everything he owned in this enterprise, met me at the door of what would become The Laconia Daily Sun. We stood for a few seconds then we walked in together. Our newly leased rooms were in the bowels of a red brick building in the center of town. There were three rooms; the news room, his office and my office. The furniture consisted of wall-to-wall carpeting, a dark brown, brush-painted newspaper stand with a telephone on top of it and ... well, that was it.

From there, we were to build a daily newspaper to compete with the hundred-year-old competition based for decades down the street a block from us. We didn't do much the first day but talk about what we would have to buy. With each addition to the list I saw Ed cringe. We decided to go shopping in the world of second-hand furniture in a few days, and then we would talk about the date for the first edition.

Within a few weeks, Lin and I bought a condo, three floors, three balconies, each with a view of Paugus Bay, a swimming pool, a tennis court and a private beach across the street. While I was at work the next week, Lin bought a hot tub. She had to bring in a 120-foot crane to lift it over the pine trees and lower it down to the deck, take off the French doors, take the tub apart and reassemble it inside the family room. Stuff just didn't get in Lin's way when she decided to do something.

It seemed we had dodged another bullet. The condo was inexpensive and the land was magnificent. The morning after we bought our new place to live, we walked out to Weirs Beach. The totally iced in lake was nestled in the arms of the mid winter haze that slid down the sides of the surrounding mountains. The fog crossed the lake, and, like a Steven King novel, it rolled down the streets into town. Some force had to be propelling it, but if so it was invisible.

The banks of Winnipesaukee at Weirs Beach was lined by a quaint row of closed shops. Standing at the entrance to the idle "fun center," a vacation haven for teens, we leaned against each other and took in the snow-covered Mount Washington in the distance.

As the spring progressed we watched the snow cover melt away, the white cap climbing up the sides of the mountain. We also watched with anticipation for the state of the lake known to the locals as "ice out."

But until then, we watched the ice fishing huts on the lake with smoke trickling out the chimneys on top. Trucks parked beside each, men and boys being brought lunch by their women. The days were still cold but warming, and the first edition went out. Lin had sold enough ads to pay for its production costs.

The drive up Gunstock Mountain, where tourists came to ski, presented a beautiful panorama of forest, church steeples, and small enclaves of houses below and a perfectly white and snow filled sky above. And the air was fresh, like we had never smelled before. There were scenic lookouts in our neighborhood, and we drove out on Sundays, drank our morning coffee sitting in the Jeep with the engine running, watching the sunlight creep softly across the snow covered valley. The deer and moose weren't shy and made morning visits to watch us drink our coffee and eat our donuts. Even a few black bears spent an occasional morning there with us.

Day after day the sky was a winter white and the kind of snow that falls the day before Christmas, clean and so white it shone blue at dusk, fell nearly every day. Every farm with expansive white fields and split rail fences looked like a post card.

Then, as the snow melted and the shops began to open like flowers greeting the spring we found something else.

For the most part, the people were ugly, filled with hate and anger.

It turned out that for a hundred years working class families had vacationed here and dropped off their energy of frustration for having only a week or two before returning to work. They left, and another family took their place, dropping off their own anger and tension with life. It seemed that the mountains surrounding the lake kept the energy in place and it permeated the lives of everyone who chose to live here.

The economy of this north country haven hinged its livelihood on one horrible week of the deep throated roar of Harleys and old Indians and the nasty rattle of Suzukis, Hondas and Yamahas – The beautiful but helpless valley was inundated with 350,000 motorcycles, the smell of overcrowded beer tents, the exhilaration of Jello shots from a naked stomach, and drunkenness, debauchery, gang fights, traffic gridlock and every form of mayhem and nonsense you ever experienced or even heard of. And vendors selling T-shirts on the side of the road in full view of every kid in the city. The slogans were "If you can read this the bitch fell off," and its partner T-shirt "I'm the bitch." Or on the roadside you could buy a shirt that proclaimed "Fuckin Donuts."

But Bike Week wouldn't come until next June, pretty much the same week the local high schools would hold graduation, and another batch of 18 year olds would be dropped into the welcoming and drunken arms of Motorcycle Week in Laconia.

A column I wrote during Bike Week, stated, "I have friends and family who ride motorcycles. I even have friends who are full-fledged members of motorcycle gangs. I love them all, love to see them, but not all at once."

It was as if the devil had taken up residence in paradise.

I jumped into building a newspaper, and Lin enrolled in the Dove Star Institute learning how to be a massage therapist. I was seriously impressed when her courses covered more biology and anatomy than I had ever seen. She drove to school five days a week, wrote feature stories at night and a few days a week she sold ads for the paper. With her two-hour drive to and from the school on I-93, and four or five stories a week while jumping from store to store explaining why it would be worth someone's while to buy an ad in a fledgling newspaper, I had the decidedly better deal.

"The window in my office was on a level with the wheels of the cars in the parking lot, so when the snow melted it found an escape in through my window and a home on my floor. That morning I had read a few emails and invited the writers to meet me in my office that day so I had to get a shop vac and vacuum up the floor. I stood in an inch of water while I was making coffee and Ed came in, jokingly called me some names, grabbed the plug to the Mr. Coffee, and pulled it out of the outlet.

"Don't kill yourself yet. I can't do this by myself." He smiled.

My morning appointments arrived and with a smile and a nod for my new boss, I ushered them into my office. The taller one with the red hair was a Jewish man from a nearby temple. He clutched our newspaper from a week earlier and a Lipton cup-of-soup. He looked warily at the other man as he sat down. The second was a young bearded man who was as dark as people were allowed to get in Laconia by environment and heredity. He wore silver wire-rimmed glasses, which upon sitting he immediately took off and cleaned so as not to have to look at anyone in the room.

"I thought we'd be alone," he said to me but looking across at the other man. I could tell they knew each other.

"Well, it didn't work out that way, did it?" I answered without trying to hide my disappointment with their accusations.

Both men – the Jew and the Palestinian had complained that I was "blatantly" taking the other's side in a column I had written about neither of them.

"Can you explain why this is a group meeting?" the Lipton Soup asked.

"You both had the same complaint."

Both heads snapped to face each other like a set of those kissing dolls with magnets in their heads.

"I thought I would like to see your faces while I tell you what I have to tell you." I smiled.

Each man looked intently at me more to avoid the other than to pay attention to me, this new editor in a new newspaper who they seriously wanted to convert.

"You both complained that I had taken the side of the other." I said sneaking a peek at Ed who had stopped walking in the middle of the newsroom so he could look into my office. He looked like the deer I met so often on my way home at night, frightened as to what was to come next.

"So, I wanted to tell you I was not talking about either of you and, therefore, I couldn't have been favoring either or disparaging either." I stopped to let it sink in and just as the young Jewish man opened his mouth I began again.

"But I would like to say something before I ask you both to leave … You Red, I will take up your cause when you stop taking out entire neighborhoods in retribution against one man. And you sir, when you stop strapping explosives to women and allowing them to blow themselves up with the promise of taking care of her family when she is gone."

They now both looked like Ed - eyes wide, sitting stock still.

"So," I said as I rose from behind the desk, "if you two would get the fuck out of my office I can get to the important work of vacuuming the water off this floor." I turned on the vacuum. They left. Ed shook his head and smiled.

He came back with coffee for both of us and as we laughed standing in my office, The Laconia Sun was born.

In September the World Trade Center was attacked.

Chapter 41

HOW MANY OF YOU HAVE SEEN SOMEONE SHOT?

(Mandy, 25 - 30 years old)
2002-2007

"Ms. Eppley, can I ask the class a question?" Kiarra asked, swiveling in her front row seat before I had a chance to respond.

"Of course," I replied to the back of her head, grateful for her initiative.

"How many of y'all have seen someone shot?"

Every hand rose. Kiarra nodded, content with herself, but not finished. She turned back to see my hands by my side.

"What 'bout you?"

I shook my head solemnly.

"How many of y'all have seen someone shot in the head? Because that's a whole different thing."

About half of the students held their hands in the air. She looked back at me, holding my glance for a moment.

"Can I lead the discussion?"

"Go ahead," and with that, I had relinquished the control of the classroom I had only managed to garner in the past few weeks. It was the end of my first year teaching, as a Teach For America corps member in Deep East Oakland, California. John and I left DC right after getting married and moved to Berkeley for graduate school. I added a masters' degree in city and regional planning to my resume, and then decided I needed more real world experience. The world didn't get much more real than this Tuesday morning's seventh grade English/history core. Minutes before their class began yesterday, the teacher next door had casually mentioned to me that he was hearing rumors of a shooting Sunday night, and I had taught that class in a fog. An article graced Tuesday morning's *Oakland Tribune*, and despite his advice to leave it alone, I photocopied it and distributed it to my class.

The students were in the final stages of essays documenting the problems in their community. It was June, and it had been a long year. I started teaching at a different school, but when I was "consolidated" because they had too many teachers for their enrollment, a friend and mentor helped me find a position where she worked. This school had a stellar administration, but I still fought an uphill battle starting six weeks into the school year, as a brand new teacher, in an inner-city school. Through determination and a lot of support, I had finally gained some semblance of control in my classroom, and this was the first assignment during which my students had stopped fighting me and began to fully engage in class. One student, however, still rebelled against my naive wording of the assignment and had instead written a wonderfully persuasive piece highlighting what made his neighborhood so special. Tragically, that Sunday night, his oldest brother was shot and killed less than a block from their home.

As I walked around the room distributing the photocopied article, my students didn't need to look at the paper to know its contents, so instead they fixed their eyes upon mine.

"What are we going to do with this?" One student asked.

"We're going to read it," I answered with feigned confidence.

"Then what?" Another followed.

"I'm not sure," I admitted, quietly.

"Are you going to cry?" A third asked.

"I don't know," I whispered.

Most likely in an attempt to postpone that possibility as long as possible, students had volunteered to read aloud, and when we finished reading, I had instructed them to take a few minutes to jot down their reactions for themselves. I wrote as well, allowing myself the time to process along with them. When I stopped writing, I realized I was without a plan; no credentialing class could possibly prepare me for the path I had just started down. I asked if anyone wanted to share with the class, and when no one responded, Kiarra had raised her hand.

With my blessing, she led a discussion about violence in their community. Students spoke honestly and listened respectfully to each other's fears, personal tragedies, and experiences. Derrick raised his hand to speak, and when Kiarra acknowledged him he paused. With all eyes on him, he finally spoke, deliberately.

"Damn," he started, paused, and then allowed his voice to trail off. "Just damn."

The teacher who had originally told me of the news, and had advised me to skip the article and forge on with class as normal, walked past my open door at that moment, using his expression alone to admonish Derrick, who was often in trouble. I rose from my chair, quickly crossed the front of my classroom, and forcefully shut my door through the teacher's glare. Derrick had sworn at me many times that year, and I had often needed help with discipline, but this was different. We looked at each other, and I walked to the front of the classroom, ready to take control. Kiarra now turned to face me.

"Go ahead," I said gently to Derrick, and he continued through his tears.

In the end the class made cards for their friend, who returned only once that year, for the class's presentation of those community essays.

My first year teaching, which culminated at the funeral, shattered my comfort zone, and I could not wait for my second year to begin. I had finally found what my travels, my moves, my different professions and degrees had failed to produce. My students offered me a window to a world beyond my own, pulled back the thick drapes, and explained it to me.

I will be forever grateful for their patience and their respect.

Chapter 42

YOU HAVE TO KNOW WHEN
A DOG'S GOING TO BITE

(John, 57 years old)
2002

Ken, our 20-something reporter, a young man I thought had a less than an average amount of energy, was inexperienced, and wasn't even paying attention to the experience he was living. But he was inexplicably likeable. We all liked him, and more importantly the people of the town liked him. So he was a keeper.

One afternoon he stepped into my office and said, "They're here." His face was a frightened white and his eyes were wide, and he looked shaken.

"Who," Ed and I both answered.

"Hell's Angels."

"All of them?" I asked looking over his shoulder into the reception area.

"No, just one,"

"What does he want?" I asked.

"I don't know. I didn't ask him, are you crazy?"

"I guess. I got this."

I could see through the doorway to the reception area the colors on the back of the leather jacket on the young man who with his clean blond hair hanging into his eyes and his practiced grimace and his scrabbly beard could have been one of the high schoolers on my last Hopedale soccer team.

"Can I help you?" I asked.

"Sonny wants some copies of your paper."

At first I was confused. Then it dawned on me. "Oh, the one with his picture on the front?"

"Right," He actually looked embarrassed.

As I fished a handful of the papers from the stacks in the closet and handed them to him I had to laugh. "They send you for coffee too?" I smiled.

"You have no idea," he laughed. "How'd you know?"

"No rocker. You're not a member yet. So you're …"

"Right. A gopher. How much do I owe you?"

Sonny Barger, the founder of the original Oakland Chapter of Hell's Angels, was in town, and we had gotten a picture of him. This kid had been sent out to fetch some papers, and my reporter was shaking in my office.

"Nothing, man. They're free."

"He said to pay you."

"It's a free paper."

He made a face of approval and left.

I turned to the thankful, I think, gaze of our reporter.

"They're just people, Ken. I grew up with them ... before they joined a club."

"Yeah, but they kill people."

I thought for a few seconds. That was true enough, "But not if they have no reason."

Lin finished her classes and her national test, which most people flunked the first few times, and the newspaper doubled its circulation and was solid with advertising, despite the "suggestions" of the Pros from Dover who between them had six month's experience as a reporter, and who we pretty much ignored.

On a Monday morning in July, Ed called me into his office.

"I hear you and Lin are looking at houses."

I nodded knowing this was not why he had called me in.

"I'm sure you remember when you were hired I told you that when we broke even I would pay you the going rate for an editor of a daily newspaper."

I was happy to hear this since that would mean my salary would just about double.

"I remember."

"Well, this month we broke even."

It sure sounded as if there was to be a "but" in there.

"John, I have exhausted my savings ... I need to take a bigger paycheck to pay my mortgage and keep the paper going."

We both knew what that meant.

"You built a paper here that can run itself ... and I need your pay to be my pay. I need to let you go in August. I'm sorry."

This was not becoming my favorite month, but then again the last "surprise" in August turned out pretty good, so I laughed.

This of course was not what he expected.

"Ed," I said. "Don't worry. I always win."

In August I took a job with the largest newspaper in Connecticut as its wire editor and parlayed that into being an opinion columnist within a few months. We said goodbye to the Laconia Daily Sun, working 14 hour days 6 or 7 days a week, and Lin putting up with working with a chiropractor who thought he was a real doctor while she held down two other jobs at the same time.

On the week after I left the Sun, and before we left for southwestern Connecticut, we took a drive to see the land we were leaving, sort of to say goodbye.

We drove north toward Meredith and took a left into the hills. Within an hour we found ourselves on a dirt road passing an idyllic farm. As we rolled by, I looked into the browning September field of corn, the split rail fences augmented by wire, the hundred-year-old oak tree in front of the big white farm house, and the bench near the mailbox at the road where children waited for the mail to be delivered. It could have been the setting for the 1950s version of TVs Lassie.

As we rolled past, trying to keep down the dust we were kicking up, I heard a bark. We had the top up on the Wrangler, but the windows on the sides and back were off. There, behind us, was a dog, the nastiest black dog you have ever seen. It was drooling, fangs bared, eyes red and in full sprint. And it was catching us.

With thoughts of it jumping right into the back of the Jeep, I looked at Lin. We laughed, and I floored it, the dust be damned. And so ended our life in the lakes region of New Hampshire.

On to the land of the WASP.

Chapter 43
HOPEDALE, REVISITED

(Mandy, 30 - 37 years old)
2007 - 2014

"2:09. Not bad! We should be able to beat some of the traffic," I exclaimed proudly, catching my breath from the jog up the short hill to the back parking lot at the high school. Four minutes earlier I had given my honors sophomores until Monday to complete their project dividing life into seven categories and showing it in both written and illustrated form. The assignment had angered my class of bright, over-achievers, as they would be unable to check their answers in books or online. I reveled in their frustration, taking it as a sign that I had created a rare assignment that truly made them think. I switched off the light as the last student exited my room, locked the door behind them, stopped to check that my Gay Straight Alliance students had found their way into my co-advisor's room, and snuck out the back door into a sea of students.

"We have to stop back at the house," John interjected.

"Why?" I asked, and John motioned to the back of the car, where Alex, who had turned five only days before, squirmed tellingly. "Oh." We hadn't even made it onto the road yet, and we already needed a bathroom break.

"Otherwise, we're ready." John had clearly worked hard for that fact, picking Chris up early from Kindergarten at the elementary school three doors down the road, dropping Sunny, our almost two year old golden-doodle off at my mother's house, and loading the Prius with kids' bikes and the cargo box for our three-day-weekend adventure. He couldn't have gotten much work done himself.

With no help from our false start, we reached New York in the middle of rush hour, and despite a strategic dinner break, we didn't reach our Philly area hotel until nearly ten o'clock. There was no logical reason for my rush out of Hopedale, except for my own excitement about the exit. I missed being on the road, and I was starting to feel stifled in my hometown. It had been six years since I had quit the teaching job in Oakland that I loved, and we had moved back to Hopedale for some amorphous combination of reasons I'll never quite understand. Berkeley was expensive, and we hadn't figured out how to balance child care and jobs there, and we were unsure whether a basement apartment was the right place to raise a child, no matter how beautiful the view from the downhill side. In the midst of our new parent confusion, muddling our way through the first months of life with an infant, the distant promise and pleading of family offered a simple solution, and we fled. Chris was seven months old when we loaded him and Joey, who had been demoted to dog status only by Chris's birth, into the car for the trip across the country.

Upon arriving in Hopedale, we had bought a Draper-built half-duplex and John had taken a job at MIT that allowed him to work from home roughly half the time. A year later Alex was born, and despite my efforts at consulting, I became a stay-at-home mom with two boys under two. It never suited me. I started working at the local high school, my alma mater, first as a long-term sub, next as a soccer coach, then as a part-time English teacher, eventually expanding to full-time status. We sold the duplex and moved down the street into a brand new, four bedroom, 2,500-square-foot home with granite countertops, a two car garage, and a master suite. We were officially living the suburban American dream. The boys became good travelers. Annual visits to their grandparent's home in Houston taught them an early love of aviation, and summer road trips up the West Coast, south to Virginia, and north into Canada gave them an understanding of the road far beyond what I had when I was three times their age.

We stayed at a hotel the first night in Philly, and stopped by Haverford in the next morning's warm June rain to visit John's advisor and show the boys his campus. Finally, we continued to the destination for which I had concocted this trip: my fifteen year college reunion. John's had been the previous weekend, and since he knew a lot of my Swarthmore friends through Ultimate and our start-up, and because he knew it meant so much to me, we decided to go to mine instead. Over the next two days, I visited Lindsay and her family in their beautiful home near campus, attended lectures on the future of technology in education, stayed in a dorm room in Wharton hall, joined former classmates at campus parties, at a parade, and at a memorial service for classmates who have passed, including my friend, Dylan. I showed my children the beauty of my campus and the surrounding Crum woods, threw a Frisbee on Mertz Lawn, caught up with dear old friends who had travelled from near and far for the occasion. On Saturday night, after John had taken the boys to the dorm for the night, I walked Ashley to the train station at the foot of campus so she could catch a train back to her friends' house in Philly, where her husband and two sons had already retreated. As the train arrived, I started to cry, taking us both by surprise. We hugged goodbye with a promise to stay in better touch, as the demands of work, family, daily life had diminished our contact in recent years. She lived in San Francisco now. She moved there only weeks after I left Berkeley; we had crossed paths at her wedding. I walked back up McGill walk alone, letting my tears flow, and not knowing why. I stopped to sit on a Parrish Beach Adirondack chair, to catch my breath, to look up at the stars. I was grateful for so much; I had no idea I had been so unhappy. By allowing myself to remember the life I had once envisioned, I was able to begin to unravel what was missing. The next day, on the drive home, John and I brainstormed plans and places, from PhD programs to Hawai'i, where we had already agreed to move when his lab relocated the next summer, and while the boys sang along to the Indigo Girls from the backseat. I vowed not to let my friendships and my dreams fade to nothing.

The next month we spent time with dear friends in Ithaca, at Storyland and Mt. Washington in New Hampshire, and at a campground in rural Vermont. Finally, in late July, I took advantage of the teacher's summer off to fly to San Francisco. Ashley had promised that if I booked a flight, she'd find us a campsite. Unfortunately, that's easier said than done in the summer in the Bay Area, or at least that's what she claimed when telling me that instead of a campsite, she had reserved a backcountry permit. We would hike seven miles on Friday, camp at one spot, hike ten the next day, camp there, and then hike fourteen miles out on Sunday. Between John and Ashley, I had come a long way as a hiker and camper over the years, but I had never gone on an overnight backpacking trip. She assured me that she had all the gear I would need, she could carry the weight for me and lead the way.

Chapter 44
HEART ATTACKS HURT

(John, 56 - 68 years old)
2002 - 2014

Lin's business and my job provided a life in which we could live comfortably and even take in her mother and father when adverse luck and a predatory home loan meant they needed help. They were family, so we took them in, not knowing that they would never leave the house for about eight years. Then, to add to the household, a few years later we also took in Lin's youngest daughter again when she hit some hard times.

Then one morning on my daily walk, a sharp pain in my chest made me stop, turn around mid-stride and head home.

That afternoon I took a stress test and failed. About a week later I was in St. Raphael's hospital being prepped for angioplasty. With Lin sitting next to the bed I felt as comfortable as if I were sitting in a park.

When I was wheeled into the operating room I was surprised. Strangely enough, you remain awake for this heart procedure. It turned out to be a good thing.

Just a short time into the ordeal I got some unsettling news.

"You're having a heart attack," the nurse whispered to me to explain the pain I was not supposed to be experiencing.

I looked at the monitor. It showed, in black and white, the wire with a stent attached pushing up from my upper leg all the way to my heart. The doctor decided he needed to explain. "When I got to your main artery, the artery split and spiraled all the way up. It wasn't my fault."

That somehow wasn't reassuring, knowing whose fault it wasn't that I was probably about to die.

He turned away and said to a nurse, "Call a surgical team." He sounded to me so very unsure.

For him, this was supposed to have been something he had done a thousand times or more, a routine procedure, like replacing a light bulb, but now that the electricity was metaphorically about to go out he was at a loss for what to do. He stood by my side waiting for a surgical team that would most likely show up too late.

"Hey!" I demanded to the surprise of everyone in the room. All heads turned toward my prone body.

"This fucking hurts." I looked around in my stupor and found the doctor. "You," I said in my best "in charge" voice. He looked at me. "Do something! Now!"

He made a quick phone call and came back with a plan. He opened up an entryway into the artery on the other leg, went up the right side of my body and put five stents in the broken artery.

After nearly six hours on the table, all those involved decided I was going to live.

I knew all along that I was going to live because Lin was sitting in the waiting room alone, and I wasn't going to leave her to put up with this bull shit. She had put up with enough in her last marriage.

The next day when the doctor came to my room to tell me he had to "go in again" the next day, I put my foot down.

"I met you Thursday, I nearly died on Saturday, and you think I'm going to give you another shot at it on Sunday? I don't think so."

I took three days off, but since two of those days were my normal weekend I earned a reputation for being the guy who took a day off to have a heart operation and quit smoking.

Before I knew it, I had been at the **Connecticut Post** for eight years, earned 15 awards for my column, including state, regional and national ones, I was in my mid 60s and being called into a disciplinary hearing by my 23-year-old supervisor, Alisette, known to most in the newsroom as Rainbow Bright.

We met in the spacious conference room, myself, Rainbow and her boss Tad, a guy a few years my junior. Tad seemed embarrassed to be there.

"I'm sorry Mr. Hourihan, but I have to discipline you for your unprofessional actions in the newsroom," Rainbow said in her best "bossy" voice.

"Which ones?" I asked.

"When I showed you that list of the new rules on the weeklies, you said," and she looked at Tad. She ruffled through some papers in front of her on the table, and read, "That is a 'bull-shit list'."

"Yeah, it is." In every high energy newsroom I had ever been in, including this one, the word "Fuck" wasn't even a word, just punctuation. "Bull shit" was more acceptable than forgetting to say "allegedly."

I looked to Tad for a little support, but he just looked at the floor.

Things had changed. She wasn't out of line with the current rules. I was.

"We can't have that kind of talk in the newsroom." Rainbow Bright said and smiled. "OK?"

I continued to look at Tad.

"I'm going back to work, "I said and got up to leave. But before I could get out the door it just came out.

"Look ... Aliss ... both of you, I was brought up poor, by a shoe worker/boxer in a tough factory town. I have been through parking lot fights, a war, teaching in the inner city, and a bunch of decades in newsrooms - real newsrooms. My vocabulary includes the words I've learned, all of them. I swear. Get over it or fire me."

Sitting at my desk a few nights later, my work done, I decided to check out the Veterans Association benefits web page. When I read it, my sour mood lifted.

The government had finally decided that all those of us who had spent time in Vietnam had been subjected to Agent Orange, and all of us who now had diabetes and ischemic heart problems because of the effects of the defoliant would be compensated. I had both.

Not more than a week later I went to previously scheduled visits with my heart doctor, my diabetes doctor and my GP. In effect, they all said the same thing. While facing the stress of multiple deadlines every day and the constant fight of a man over 60 who was trying to keep his job past what the company felt was his expiration date, and of course the repeated extended visits from family, my doctors said it would be good if I could retire. Because of the heart condition and the diabetes, my job could kill me. They said if I retired I would live longer.

We retired.

Lin's daughter, Katie, had met her soul mate online, and, when he came out to meet her for the first time, they had run off to get married. The young-and-in-love couple left, heading for Peoria. I couldn't get the song out of my head for weeks - "We're Marching to Peoria. Peoria, Peoria."

Before long, Lin's father had passed away, and her mother had gone to live with her other daughter. Lin closed her two-location, seven-therapist massage business, and I gave my notice. Our 401ks bought a small house in the Massachusetts woods, 300 square feet. We rented a large truck and donated much of what we had owned to the Boys and Girls Clubs, and we began our new life without most of the material things we had amassed over our lifetimes. Never missed a single thing.

Family Is Family Is Family Is Family

In retirement, we became closer to ourselves, to each other, and to nature, and without having our family living in our house we became closer to them too. We stopped trying to "move up," got off the ladder and returned to the values we had grown up with, values that I had nearly lost in my ladder-crawling days of scurrying out of poverty and through middle class living. We began to study the things we had always wanted to study for no other reason than that we wanted to know them.

When, a few years later, Lin's youngest daughter came back again for the third time, we were taxed heavily, but we did what we could for six months. Family is family. We got her home from New Zealand (I was never really sure how the hell she ended up in New Zealand.) We set up an apartment for her, furnished it, got her health insurance, and taxied her wherever she needed to go, making sure she was safe, fed, had a job, had state assistance, and the baby was healthy. And we accepted her new foray into Scientology.

Then it occurred to me; it was time to get back to being us.

The mid-May rain had turned the driveway into six inches of mud as we backed out at 7 a.m. It was the fourth day in a row we had made our coffee to go so we could drive Kate and baby Rory to another appointment, this time to get food assistance for her and her newborn.

Life had become an endless string of early morning drives to get her a job at a supermarket, to take her shopping, to doctor appointments and to get state or federal help. I didn't really mind, but most of the rest of her family had pretty much refused to help her financially or any other way, and this morning was the last straw.

Lin turned from the front seat to face her daughter as we drove.

Lin and I had stopped going fishing, stopped reading, walking, travelling or even out to eat since Katie had come to live with us. We no longer had the time or the money. We had ended our own life and were busy helping her live hers and subsidizing her existence, to get it back. I had ballooned to more than 200 pounds and I was getting depressed. This was not how I wanted to end my life.

So when it began to appear that my step daughter and her newborn son were going to be an everyday and omnipresent part of our lives until I was too old to care, I made a decision.

"Yeah, we ain't doing that," I told Lin that afternoon.

I knew I wasn't the sole master of my life, but I also knew I didn't have to be the perpetual victim either. Lin agreed.

Chapter 45
UNTETHERED

(Mandy, 37 - 38 years old)
2014 - 2015

As I drove through the warm February sunshine, the steady movement of a dark object pierced its brilliant green backdrop and attracted my attention. I was early for the first game of the spring season, having left ample time to account for threats of multiple lane and exit closures on the H1 that had failed to stall traffic as predicted. For the first time since arriving in Honolulu almost eight months earlier, I anticipated a sort of reunion, this time with a team I had joined in fall and hadn't seen in two months. There would be names to remember, apartments and puppies to inquire about, new players to meet, and a position to reclaim at the center of their midfield.

I continued toward what I wrongly assumed was a stray dog, until I finally realized it was not one, but two separate bodies. Each piglet moved according to his own desire, a few feet from his friend, yet as they wallowed in the mud along the side of the driveway linking the residential neighborhood to the island's largest soccer complex, they seemed to move as one, just as indifferent to the line of cars that passed only a few feet away as the cars were to their existence in a Sunday afternoon routine. Their blissful freedom was primal; they were where they wanted to be, doing what they were born to do, together, and nothing else mattered.

I have often wondered what brought us to Hawai'i. At its simplest, the answer resides in the minutes between John's boss telling him of his impending move to the University of Hawai'i at Manoa and my instant response of "Sure" to his email titled "How do you feel about moving to Hawai'i," but no five-thousand mile family move has roots that simple. I suppose that it arose at a time in which we were poised for a major change. In the weeks preceding this decision, we had discussed options from graduate school to jobs with Teach For America in Appalachia to a year-long road trip, and we had traded our Mazda 5 for a Honda Pilot for its ability to tow a camper. Still the roots of our Hawaiian adventure run deeper. Although we moved to Hopedale when Chris was seven months old, we had our reservations at the time, and we never saw it as permanent. On the drive across the country, we vowed to try our best to make it work, but we also shared a belief that we would only be able to last until Chris and any siblings reached elementary school. This move arose as Chris worked through Kindergarten, and had a date set for a year and a half in the future, when the boys would be entering first and second grades, just as we had imagined.

I suppose the answer to the question of "why Hawai'i" can be answered in an often used quote by one of my heroes, Robert Kennedy. He ended many campaign speeches by stating that, "Some see things as they are and ask 'Why?' I dream of things that never were and ask 'Why not?'" Rather than wasting time wondering why we should move to Hawai'i, we basically threw up our hands and said, "Why not?!" I had only two experiences with Hawai'i before deciding to move. The first came in the fifth grade, when I was assigned the state for a mandatory research project, and I wrote to the Board of Tourism and received informational brochures. Second, I had once booked a last minute flight from the Bay Area for an Ultimate tournament in Waimanalo. We arrived late Friday night, camped on the beach, played Ultimate all weekend, and flew back on a red-eye Sunday night. During a bye, I stood in the surf with Kelley, my dear friend and longtime roommate, discussing how lucky we were to be exactly where we were: swimming in the Pacific, on a beautiful February day, playing a sport we love, surrounded by friends. "How did this become my life?" I had asked her.

Kelley reminded me of that scene over a couple of beers at a local bar just across the Hopedale town line on the Wednesday night when I told her of our move, a year and a half in the making. It all made sense. Hawai'i just may have been the perfect place to do what I wanted to do, where I was meant to be.

We moved in June, and we fell in love with the island almost immediately. After a lifetime of seeking proximity to both the urban and natural environments, access to parks and coffee shops, mountains and museums, we found such a combination in Honolulu. The boys had new lizards and bugs to investigate, we had a rainforest to explore, and stress seemed to melt away as soon as we submerged ourselves in the crystal clear ocean. Alex danced in the Nutcracker behind a symphony orchestra, I accompanied Chris's class to a top rated museum, only a few miles from our house, and we lived close enough to enjoy take-out Ethiopian food for the first time in years. We enrolled the kids in a wonderful elementary school, where their education spans indoors to outdoors effortlessly, with teachers seemingly hand-picked for each: Alex's is a veteran who has met him where he is and challenged him to thrive while accepting his own mistakes as part of the process, Chris's shares his love of nature and welcomed his pet lizard into her classroom. I found a soccer league that I enjoy, and we both joined the vibrant Ultimate community on the island. John loves his job, and I have recently done work for an impressive charter middle school, run by a new friend, with a mission that merges sustainability and project-based learning. We have begun learning Hawaiian culture and traditions, thanks in large part to the program run by the kids' school. Shamas serenade us over dinner, and brilliant green parakeets fly by and rest in our papaya trees. We are wearing shorts and tank tops, biking to school, enjoying a morning jog, while the house we own in Massachusetts is buried under seven feet of snow. While we miss our many friends and family members, my dad and Lin moved to Waikiki, allowing us to strengthen our relationships with them and to build a deeper mutual understanding than we ever have. None of us regrets this move or has anything other than fondness for our island home, but still, we have no intentions of staying.

Life here has served its purpose. It allowed us to slow down, to find our own way, to remember what matters to us, to hear our own voices more clearly. It has untethered us from Hopedale and reminded us to make the most of every minute of our lives. It has simplified our inevitable return home, to the Bay Area, finally allowing us the freedom to enjoy where we want to be, to do what we want to do, together. I only wish that upon our arrival there, I would be able to say that nothing else would matter. Unfortunately, life may only be that simple for feral piglets. It's up to us to make the most of its wild ride.

Chapter 46
FULL CIRCLE

(John, 68 years old)
2014 - 2015

This time, when the plane landed at Honolulu Airport, I got off, looked around, and remembering the last time I was here, I laughed. If you can scrimp and save in the woods in Massachusetts, you can do the same on the beach in Honolulu.

Lin and I stood in the baggage claim area waiting for our bags to be regurgitated from the hole in the wall onto the shiny metal carousel.

"Hey," she said.

I turned to see the biggest smile I had seen since we cruised in the Caribbean on our honeymoon.

"We live in Hawai'i," she said, and the smile got bigger.

My son-in-law's job had moved from MIT to the University of Hawai'i, and he, my daughter and two of our grandchildren were going with the job. We joked with them about how we were going to accompany them. We were both a little worried about how the kids would take leaving everyone they knew except their parents, and Lin said we should lock the house and go.

So we did.

Actually we went before them and met them at the airport when they landed.

Weeks later, sitting on the beach where Duke Kahanamoku used to surf, picking at a rice and fish plate lunch, I thought about the progress of my life, from the wind near the railroad tracks in Worcester, through the barrio in South Phoenix, across Vietnam, through middle class, and the disintegration of my family, to sitting on this beach with the woman who brought me back from the dead. It had taken me a lifetime to get here, and my daughter and her family were already here. It was uplifting to know that, although I could expect this to most likely be the pinnacle for me and Lin, my daughter and her family could anticipate further progress. For them, God willing, it was about half way.

I had traded hours in front of a TV for long walks down Waikiki with Lin. I had learned how to use the new medications my doctor gave me to calm the angina so I could exercise and spent some time on the stationary bike on the recreation deck of Discovery Bay. I had even walked up a hiking trail with my grandchildren, thanks to nitroglycerine.

I had been reading a lot over the past few years at home and while vacationing on Cape Cod; Dan Brown's *The DaVinci Code* and *Inferno,* James Twyman's *Emissaries of Light*, and a trilogy by Whitley Schreiber, *Communion, Transformation* and *Confirmation*. Pretty much, the books centered on telling our human history in a non-traditional way, how we can use forces of light, energy and nature to cause the world to change for the better. Also there were the concepts that there very well may be extraterrestrials who made us into their image and likeness and are even now dictating our lives ... that they are guiding us ... and I started thinking, doesn't this sound a lot like the Bible?

I kept asking myself, "What the hell is the truth?"

It occurred to me now, shirtless on a warm beach, with the trade winds blowing across the mountains and down to the necklace of sand and black volcanic rock, among the sailboats, catamarans, surfers, paddle boarders and the parasailers that my grandchildren called multi-colored airborne jellyfish, that I had heard all this before.

One morning while we were sitting on Kuhio Beach, I watched the ocean swell and recede, and my mind wandered back to the third or fourth grade at St. Mary's Grammar School.

"Class," announced Sister John Edward, "We have a surprise for you this morning."

All of our enquiring, thirsty eyes turned to the door. Standing in the doorway had been Sister Superior in her black and white habit, the oldest and shortest nun I had ever seen. She was small and frail, and smiling ear to ear as if she were clutching the Holy Grail itself. Her thick-framed practical glasses hung on a gold chain from around her neck, and with both hands she cradled a St. Mary's-blue loose-leaf binder.

"Sister is going to read to us this morning."

The elderly nun positioned a chair before us in the middle of the high-ceilinged room. She smiled at us, then looking down to her lap she opened the binder and began to read.

That morning, and every morning for the rest of the week, this beautiful sister of the order of St. Joseph changed everything we believed in. She told us how Mary Magdalene was not a prostitute, what Jesus did from 12 years old to 30, how there was much more involved in the Fallen Angels than we had been told, and not just how, but why, history says there was a flood, and so many more new ideas that we sat mouths opened and in awe of the hugeness of religion and the history of our own kind.

Now, sitting on this Honolulu beach, I realized she had been reading to us from the Dead Sea scrolls before anyone had told her not to.

As I held Lin's hand and thought about this day so long ago, I realized a lot of what I had been reading lately was not just science fiction. It was the same history as Sister Superior had read to us in 1953. The difference was mostly semantics.

I nudged Lin.

"Hey, let's head back."

We were about a mile from our studio apartment and stopped at the Mei Mei, a local hole in the wall with great food. We ordered chicken and bitter melon with a scoop of rice because it was "good for us" and sat at the small wooden table and ate our healthy lunch.

I talked all the way through lunch and on the walk home. Then we sat on our couch and loaded the kindle and our computers with as many of the scriptures found at Nag Hamadi or Qumran that we could find, the books that were tossed out in the fifth century when the current Bible was being born. Until then these books had been called scripture. I was determined to learn about our history as a species, and since these religious books went further back than any history books I thought we could start there. The list included the Book of Enoch, the Epic of Gilgamesh, the gospels of Thomas, Mary Magdalene, Judas, The Apocalypse of Adam, and several other Christian, Buddhist, and Hindu writings, and we dug deep into our spirituality as if it wasn't just religion but the very history of this current version of human beings.

By February, when we decided to head back to the mainland in April, I felt more myself than I had since I climbed backwards down a small hill on the other side of a fence in the backyard of our Worcester tenement when I was three years old to feel the wind from the train. The world, once again, made sense to me, and the anger was finally gone. Hawai'i it turns out, with its amazing diversity, and its calm weather gives everyone who visits it a clear sense of self.

I sat with my daughter Mandy at a coffee shop and told her what I had found out through my readings and my life, and with the help of Lin's extensive knowledge of the Bible, about, well, everything.

"It's a circle." I told her, realizing that she could never agree with this, not yet. "Each life, each generation, each version of humanity, is a circle. But it only returns to the beginning if you hold onto your principles, morals and your own set of rules that you go by religiously, otherwise it spirals off endlessly. At that point where the circle completes, you can progress as a person, a generation, or a new version of humanity. But if you lose your way, the circle never completes, and there is no progress until it does. And it seems the most definite way to lose your path is to trade your individual values and family values for money, things and status."

I had found my angel, and I had met my daughter.

My circle was complete. I was ready to progress.

"Jesus said, 'The man old in days will not hesitate to ask a small child seven days old about the place of life, and he will live. For many who are first will become last, and they will become one and the same'." - **The Gospel of Thomas**

MY RULES

For many years various people had been telling me how I had lived by a set of rules that were different from the rest of the world, rules that I had most often adhered to religiously, so in an attempt to get back to the values I had felt were essential, I wrote them down.

- A person stands up for what is right.
- Family is self. Never turn your back on family.
- All's fair in love. Nothing is fair in war.
- Don't let defeat stop you.
- Refuse to be dismissed.
- Be sure you're right, then go ahead.
- Treat everyone with respect until they show you they don't deserve respect.
- Don't bully. Don't be bullied.
- Don't rat on your friends.
- Just because people are different doesn't mean they are wrong.
- Tell the truth whenever you can. When you can't tell the truth try to come close.
- Before you do something, know what you will do next.
- Treat others how you want them to treat you.
- All people are equal until they prove otherwise – either way.
- Play fair and fight fair, but win.
- No one plays nice when they are losing, so be careful when you are winning.
- Earn your money, and pay what you owe.

- Age in itself is not a reason to respect people. Some old people are assholes.
- Don't take what isn't yours, unless the one who has it doesn't own it either.
- Play the cards you're given.
- If you aren't hurting people or the planet you aren't doing anything wrong.
- Never follow a plan that ends with, "Then run like hell."
- Forgive.
- If you got yourself into it, there is a way out of it.
- Better to be the brains of the outfit than the other end.
- Know which people want to go with you, and which just want you to pay the way.
- Don't make up bad stuff about people.
- Sex is not a sin. It's a gift.
- Only follow other people's rules if they don't contradict what is right.
- God is real. So is Jesus. There are probably more.